How Does God Fit Into My Life?

Compiled from Teenage Magazine

Teenage BOOKS

Group Books

Loveland, CO

How Does God Fit Into My Life?

First Printing

Credits
Edited by Eugene C. Roehlkepartain
Designed and illustrated by Judy Atwood Bienick
Cover design by RoseAnne Buerge
Cover photo by Joe Coca

The material in this book previously appeared in TEENAGE Magazine, formerly called GROUP MEMBERS ONLY Magazine.

Library of Congress Cataloging-in-Publication Data
How does God fit into my life?
1. Teenagers—Religious life. 2. Teenagers—Conduct of life. I. Teenage magazine (Loveland, Colo.)
BV4531.2.H595 1989 248.8'3 89-4562
ISBN 0-931529-87-5

Printed in the United States of America

Contents

Part Two: **Making Room for God**

Introduction

How Does God Fit Into Your Life?

Suppose God snapped his fingers and you found yourself standing at heaven's entrance. You try opening the pearly gates, but they're locked. After a while, the gatekeeper arrives, looks you over and checks his roster.

He then announces: "Before you can enter, we must find out how much God was a part of your life on Earth. Therefore, you must pass a test. Let's return to Earth, and you can give me a tour of your bedroom. If I see God's presence in your room, we'll open heaven's gates and let you in."

Your mouth drops open. This must be a nightmare! Who is this jerk anyway?

You can't believe he wants to barge into your bedroom—the only place on Earth where you can let it all hang out. And he wants to search for evidence of God?

You feel sunk. You wish somebody would pinch you, and you could get out of this. If this is heaven, what's hell like?

► Sitting on the Hot Seat

You wake up and shake your head. You look around and you realize, thank goodness, that your nightmare was a dream. You relax and reach over to turn on the stereo, which is tuned to a top-40 station. You begin tapping your foot to the beat.

Suddenly you hear a knock at the door.

You get up and turn down the music. You open the door and gasp. Standing outside your bedroom door, with clipboards and TV cameras, is the fearsome fivesome.

"I'm Mike Wallace."

"I'm Morley Safer."

"I'm Harry Reasoner."

"I'm Ed Bradley."

"I'm Diane Sawyer."

"And this is *60 Minutes*."

And you feel sick.

Mike Wallace clears his throat and glares at you over the rim of his reading glasses. He pulls out volumes of notes and begins flipping through them. You begin to sweat.

"We understand you're the teenager in this household." he says. "We'd like to ask some questions about how God fits into your life. And we'd like to start by looking around your bedroom."

Terrifying images flash through your mind. What did you do with your sweaty gym socks? your dirty underwear? What about that steamy paperback you borrowed?

And those album covers and posters on your wall. You gulp. One poster says, "Talk Dirty to Me." You hadn't noticed it until now.

Where are Petra and Stryper when you need them? your scout ribbons? Where's that little pocket Bible Grandma gave you?

Where's a hole you can crawl into?

► Exploring Bill's Room

Fortunately, you can relax. Just as the *60 Minutes* crew is about to fire the first question, Mike Wallace receives a phone call about another urgent assignment. The crew has to leave immediately.

You got lucky. But my friend Bill didn't. When I decided to investigate his room, I didn't get any phone calls beckoning me to an urgent assignment.

Bill wasn't expecting my visit. He didn't know why I wanted to take a whirlwind tour of his bedroom. But he agreed anyway.

When I reached his bedroom door, a poster with big, red letters grabbed my attention:

THIS ROOM HAS BEEN DECLARED A HYSTERICAL LANDMARK

I knew I was in for an adventure.

The first thing that caught my eye when I walked into his room was a dart board. In the middle of the board was a girl's photograph. A dart stuck out from the girl's forehead. Bull's-eye!

"It seems you two have some problems," I said.

"Yeah," Bill shrugged. "I got dumped." He laughed and added, "She'll come to her senses."

Album covers and rock music posters covered Bill's walls. Stacks of Sports Illustrated, Inside Running, Club and something called Circus magazine lined his bookcases. Yearbooks and photo albums lay in a heap.

On a bulletin board, I noticed a cross made out of nails on a piece of wood.

"That's interesting," I said, fingering the rows of nails.

"That was a vacation Bible school project," Bill said. "A long time ago."

I turned it over. I noticed a beverage can's tab top on the back to attach it to the wall. "That's clever," I remarked.

Bill laughed self-consciously. "I took it off a beer can. Kind of weird, huh?"

I didn't ask any more questions about it. I hung the cross of nails back on the wall. Then I noticed a Bible lying by Bill's bed amidst coins, pens, scratch paper and a couple of paperbacks. I asked him if he reads the Bible.

He quickly replied that he did every night.

"Come on now," I teased. "Tell me the truth."

"Well, almost every night. Maybe more like every other night. Depends on how awake I am."

► Examining the Evidence

I left Bill's room with more questions than I had gone in with. I thought about the bizarre-looking characters on his walls. The paperbacks and magazines. And the Playboy I spied near the bottom of the bookcase.

If I were Mike Wallace, could I fairly report to millions of TV viewers about how much God is a part of Bill's life? If I were heaven's gatekeeper, would the bedroom tour tell me enough about Bill's faith to grant or deny him entry into heaven?

Bill's room shows that life offers a zillion choices. And all these choices can be confusing and difficult. Every day conflicting choices bombard us. That's life. And the choices you make recall how you fit God into your living.

► A Tour of Your Life

This book takes you on a tour—not just of your bedroom but of your life. How does God fit into what you do every day?

Your school.
Your work.
Your dating.
Your pocketbook.
Your music choices.

The first part of this book looks at these issues, giving you a chance to evaluate how God fits into each area. Then the second part of the book gives you some practical ideas of ways you can make room for God in your life.

Prayer.
Going to church.
Bible study.
Helping other people.

► Your Own Tour

Before you begin exploring all these areas, though, tour your own bedroom. Try this exercise:

- Use the diagram on the facing page to sketch your room from a bird's-eye perspective.
- Add all your furniture—your bed, your desk (if you can find it), your dresser and anything else you have.
- Then note what you have on the walls and in different places in the room. Include posters, pictures, your stereo, books, musical instruments, clothes closets, makeup kits, a telephone, a computer—whatever you have.
- Now, look at your picture. What does it tell you about yourself and your priorities, hobbies and interests? Write what you learn:

- What do you *like* about your room?

- What signs do you see of how God fits into your life (a Bible, a youth group calendar and so forth)?

- What would you like to change about your room?

Look at the tough choices you make. They present some snarls you must untangle. Maybe

Tour Guide to My Room

(A Bird's-Eye View)

you'll want to do some housecleaning. But remember: God already fits into your life. He's part of your world, no matter how many "No Trespassing" signs you hang up.

► What's Really Important

Of course, a tour of your bedroom isn't really the best way to find out how God fits into your life. All I saw by touring Bill's bedroom was its outward appearance. I only looked at the many fragments of his life. I shouldn't decide whether I see God in Bill's life. What matters is what's in Bill's heart.

In 2 Peter 1:3, it says, "God's divine power has given us everything we need to live a truly religious life through our knowledge of the one who called us to share in his own glory and goodness."

Okay, grit your teeth and think. What does this verse mean? Look at the word "live." It's a verb. Living is an act of doing.

How do you deal with all the clutter in your life? In Bill's room we saw how Bill loves and how he hates. The girl he loves dumps him, so he pokes her picture full of holes.

So instead of asking, "How does God fit into your bedroom?" maybe we need to rephrase the question to put it in a clearer perspective.

Is your living fit for God?

Think about it. And explore the question through the chapters in this book.

Tom Tozer

Part One

Is There Room for *God?*

Chapter 1

You Hypocrite!

How does God fit into your lifestyle?

"So you call yourself a Christian and you're proud of it," says a friend. "I'd be embarrassed to be a Christian. You know what happened to Mike? He said he was born again. But it took him only two months to get two Christian girls pregnant."

You're stumped.

You don't know how to respond. He's right. Mike did get two Christian girls pregnant. Mike did say he was born again. And Mike's example bothers you too.

So what can you say? What can you tell people about Christianity when you know hypocrites lurk in your youth group and in your church? And you even admit feeling a bit hypocritical now and then.

What's worse, prominent Christian leaders sometimes have personal lifestyles that cause a lot of head-shaking, raised eyebrows, laughter and ridicule. They've given all the "I told you so" people another chance to put Christians on the firing line.

You have enough headaches trying to keep your own Christian values intact. You don't need other Christians messing things up. While you're trying to overcome temptations, some of today's most powerful and influential Christian leaders are giving in to temptation. This double standard makes your Christian life even tougher to live.

But don't expect it to get any easier. People will always challenge you. They'll scrutinize what you say and the way you act. They'll evaluate the way you dress, groom yourself and act in a crowd. That's because people love to catch you when you make a wrong turn. It underscores all their doubts and skepticisms about Christianity.

The tough part is realizing that you'll make a lot of wrong turns. We all do. Christians aren't immune to making incredible blunders.

But some people expect Christians to be perfect. That's because they don't understand what Christianity is all about.

So how do you handle the intimidating challenges people set before you? What should you say when people point to prominent Christians and ask how they can be such big-time Christians and such big-time sinners at the same time? What do you do if others call you a hypocrite? Try one of these approaches.

► Agree With Them

After all, they're right. There's no use arguing

Wearing the Best Face

Your dad wants to know why you came home two hours after curfew. You tell him you had car trouble when, in reality, you were at your girlfriend's house. Her parents weren't home. You figure one small lie won't hurt you or your dad.

Situations like this happen to all of us. We each put on our best face so we don't look so bad. We twist the truth, and we think it's okay.

But actually, we're not only lying but we're also being hypocrites. We're pretending to be what we aren't. We're not being honest.

Take a look at this list. Study each pair of words, one in the left column and the one directly across from it in the right column. Then think of a situation in which you wore a good face to cover up a bad face.

The Good Face	The Bad Face
Honest	Cheating
Sincere	Insincere
Enjoying yourself	Bored
Concerned	Apathetic
Serious	Laughing inside
Praying	Daydreaming
Unselfish	Looking out for #1
Being a friend	Being a phony

Choose one set of words that give you the most trouble in your daily life. Make a pledge to stop that particular act of hypocrisy. Pray for God's help.

the point. Christians are human too. In fact, the Pharisees even viewed Jesus as a hypocrite. They thought if he was truly the Son of God, he wouldn't hang around with such outcasts. But Jesus ministered to all kinds of people. He didn't handpick a group of perfect people to be with. He called together the sinners, the sick and the downtrodden people who you and I probably would have a hard time welcoming into our church.

In Matthew 4, Jesus spent time with epileptics, paralytics and people possessed by demons. In Matthew 11, he hung out with non-believers. And in John 8, he spent time talking with an adulteress.

Jesus sat with these people. He ate with them and comforted them. He prayed with them. And he befriended them.

Being a Christian doesn't mean looking down at people we think are inferior. It means recognizing that all people are God's children. So that means if you know a picked-on teenager who eats alone, join him or her. Jesus didn't worry about what the Pharisees thought. He knew the so-called outcasts needed a friend.

Because we're human, we'll occasionally look down on some people. We'll sin. But we can ask for forgiveness, learn from our mistakes and grow as Christians.

► Challenge Them

Some people love to find Christian impostors. And they love to lump all Christians into a wad of hypocrites.

But don't let them. Instead, ask them the following questions:

- If you saved money and discovered a few counterfeit bills in the stack, would you throw out all the money you saved?
- If you discovered that one pair of your designer jeans was actually a cheap imitation, would you burn all your jeans?
- If you found one small, brown spot in a banana, would you throw out the entire bunch?

Now what about Christians? Just because one or two nationally known preachers admit they've committed adultery doesn't mean all Christians commit adultery. And just because a teenager on the youth council gets drunk doesn't mean all Christian teenagers do.

So when people criticize Christians, don't hesitate to stand up for your faith. Explain that Christianity isn't a museum for displaying saints. It's a hospital for sinners. And most Christians quickly admit they have a lot of growing to do.

► Welcome Them

Throw a curve to non-Christians. Invite them to your church or youth group. Make it clear, however, that you and your Christian friends don't accept perfect people. Caution those you invite that they may run into a few egotists in your group. But tell them to expect to meet some terrific Christians who're trying to become even more terrific.

Also explain that they'll meet some "free" people. These people accept themselves as less than perfect. They feel free to share their struggles, dreams and pain. Then ask them how many people they know who remove their masks to show who they really are.

► Love Them

Regardless of what people say, love them. As a Christian, that's your job. It's easy to become smug and say non-Christians don't know what they're missing. It's tempting to rub their faces in the mud when they hurt you and call you names.

But what does Jesus say in Luke 6:27-28? "But I tell you who hear me: Love your enemies, do good to those who hate you, bless those who curse you, and pray for those who mistreat you."

So love them. Although they may make you angry, keep loving them. Don't be concerned about them judging you. Instead, make sure you don't judge them. As Jesus says in Matthew 7:4-5: "How dare you say to your brother, 'Please, let me take that speck out of your eye,' when you have a log in your own eye? You hypocrite! First take the log out of your own eye, and then you will be able to see clearly to take the speck out of your brother's eye."

► Be Yourself

It's easy to "cast the first stone" when you see Christian hypocrites. But remember what Jesus said? Only a sinless person should cast a stone. And once you start to look at yourself, it's obvious you're not perfect.

Jesus' View of Hypocrites

So what does the Bible say about hypocrites? A lot. And most of its wise words come from Jesus himself.

Read each of the following Bible passages. Write the reason Jesus was concerned about hypocrites. Then write the advice he gives.

Scripture Passage	Jesus' Concern	Jesus' Advice
Matthew 6:5-13		
Matthew 6:16-18		
Matthew 23:1-29		
Mark 7:1-13		
Luke 6:37-42		
Luke 12:1-3		
Luke 12:54-56		

So know who you are—shortcomings and all. Know what you believe and what you don't. Be honest about your strengths and weaknesses.

But even if you do those things, it's tempting to point fingers at bad Christians. How can you be yourself without judging others?

- ***Don't let others shake your faith.*** Don't let someone heap all Christians' sins on your shoulders. Don't let someone make you feel guilty about who you are and what you believe.

Someone already took the sins of the world upon his shoulders. Christ already accepts you the way you are—scars and all. You're loved. Forgiven. Free.

- ***Please God, not others.*** It doesn't matter what others say or think about you. That's hard to swallow. But as your faith grows stronger, you'll realize that if you live your life to please others, you'll have no life of your own.

Once you make up your mind to please God instead of others, know that life won't always be easy. Cynics and label-makers will constantly challenge you. At times they may ignore, ridicule and even persecute you. But Christians always face these things because of their beliefs.

- ***Live your life like Jesus lived his.*** He was called a blasphemer. People laughed at him and called him names. Eventually they nailed him to a cross and suspended him between two thieves to suffer an agonizing death.

But how did Jesus respond? He didn't give in to the crowds. His life was more important than battling ridiculers. And so is yours.

Tom Tozer

Chapter 2

I Was Turning People Off

How does God fit into your relationships?

"I'd like to speak with you alone," my science teacher told me. "Will you step outside?"

I followed him out of the classroom into a secluded storage area. I couldn't imagine what he wanted to talk to me about.

"I'll be as tactful as possible," he started. "You need to stop hounding others about Christianity. I've received complaints."

What? Hounding others? I couldn't believe it. My science teacher—a Christian I adored—was accusing me of sharing my Christianity.

► Turning Others Off

"They say you're bothering them all the time

by reading the Bible and preaching. Greg Marley's mother even talked to the principal because she says you're violating her son's civil rights."

Civil rights? What was she talking about? I didn't know how to respond.

My teacher continued: "The principal agreed someone would talk with you. He asked me to do it."

"I—I don't understand," I stammered. I felt hurt and defensive. Tears welled up in my eyes.

"Your English teacher complained that you told him in front of 30 students that he shouldn't have his radio tuned to a rock-music station because of Proverbs 15:26. He said you also condemn alcoholic beverages because of Proverbs 23:29-31 and those who swear because of James 5:12. Is that true?"

"Well, yes," I admitted. "But that's what God says, isn't it? You believe it, don't you? I just wanted Mr. Forrest to read the Bible. He's not a Christian."

"But, Dawn, do you believe he'll listen to you if you condemn his music and embarrass him in front of his students?"

"I—I don't know," I said. "When you put it that way, I guess not."

"Look, Dawn," my teacher said gently. "I know you're excited about being a Christian. You want others to be too. But you're turning people off. I hope you'll try another approach."

► Meeting Others' Needs

My science teacher was right. People knew me

Are You a Christian Snob?

It's human nature to cut others down to build yourself up and to condemn others for breaking your standards. But feeling superior and putting down other people are symptoms of a disease that's worse than having celery strings stuck between your teeth. The disease is judgmentalism.

Are you a judgmental person? Take this quick self-test to see. Mark each statement "Yes" or "No."

Do I ever judge people by . . .

- how they look? Yes ☐ No ☐
- the color of their skin? Yes ☐ No ☐
- how they talk? Yes ☐ No ☐
- who their friends are? Yes ☐ No ☐
- where they live? Yes ☐ No ☐
- the school they attend? Yes ☐ No ☐
- the church they go to? Yes ☐ No ☐
- their age? Yes ☐ No ☐
- the country they come from? Yes ☐ No ☐
- their past mistakes with no reference to how they live now? Yes ☐ No ☐
- their interests? Yes ☐ No ☐
- their intelligence? Yes ☐ No ☐
- their clothes? Yes ☐ No ☐
- what their parents do for a living? Yes ☐ No ☐
- what classes they attend? Yes ☐ No ☐
- the house they live in? Yes ☐ No ☐

continued

Did you have any "yes" answers? If so, you're a bona fide judgmentalist. And that's not surprising, since everyone's judgmental in some ways at some times.

But you can do something about it. Here are some cures for judgmentalism:

- **Remember you're not God.** God sees people for who they really are; you don't. Condemning isn't in your job description. "Do not judge, lest you be judged" (Matthew 7:1) is pretty simple advice.

- **Separate the inner person from the person's actions.** You can dislike what someone does, while still caring about that person (John 7:24).

- **Forget the popular status scale of who's inferior and who's superior.** God loves Christians and non-Christians. Although your ego may fight the idea, God regards each of us equally.

- **Use judgment, not judgmentalism.** The people we label don't need more put-downs. They need friendship, recognition, guidance and emotional support. Christians who sin need care and help to put things back together (Galatians 6:1-2). Non-Christians need Christ, not condemnation. Practice good judgment and constructive criticism.

Bill Stearns

around school for my witness overkill. I used the Bible as a weapon to point out others' faults, but I rarely ministered to their needs.

I thought I was doing the right thing. Whenever there was a sin to condemn, a wrong to right or a commandment to apply, I did it. And the classmates who didn't laugh their heads off whenever I was around hated me.

Don't make the same mistake I did. You can be a Christian without having people hate you.

► Sharing Your Faith

You can share your faith with others while continuing to grow on your own.

- ***Ask for God's help.*** Realize that God has a plan for you. And you can influence others for him. (See Jeremiah 29:11-12.)
- ***Be a good friend.*** Be kind to others without showing favoritism (James 2:1). Help others as often as you can (Proverbs 17:17).
- ***Keep a positive attitude.*** Be a conscientious student and a school leader (Philippians 2:5 and Colossians 3:17). Live a life that wins the respect of others (1 Thessalonians 4:11-12).
- ***Don't give in to peer pressure.*** Stand up for what you know is right, even when it seems you're all alone (1 Corinthians 10:13).
- ***Remember you're not better than others.*** Being a Christian doesn't make you a better person, just a forgiven person. Don't think you know all the answers to the world's questions (1 Corinthians 4:7).

Dawn Korth

The ABCs of Friendship

Friendship is more than doing things together, more than phoning someone to go to a movie or to play tennis. True friendship is based on respect and involvement; on trying to understand our friends' feelings as much as—and sometimes more than—we understand our own. A friend is someone we know we can turn to without excuses and without fear.

Being a good friend is as simple as ABC:

Always keep a confidence. Everyone needs somebody to confide in—someone to listen to our innermost thoughts, feelings, fears—and, yes, even our mistakes. However, we also need to know that our close friend understands what it means to keep a trust.

A good friend respects the difference between information that can be passed on to others and confidences that are meant to be withheld. The "friend" who spreads bad news is a gossip, wanting to show off that he or she is privy to juicy tidbits. If you want to be a good friend, then you'll keep confidences.

continued

Be supportive. Over lunch, Doug told his friend Mike about a problem he was having with his parents. It seemed to Doug that his mom and dad just couldn't understand he was old enough to use the family car; he felt they treated him like a baby.

Like a good friend, Mike listened. Then he told Doug how he had experienced a similar problem. He didn't say: "Oh, don't be silly. You're making a big deal out of nothing. Everything will be okay." He understood the second rule of friendship.

Care for your friends. Nancy's father died. Lori felt uncomfortable and didn't know how to approach Nancy. So she pretended nothing had happened. Kris, on the other hand, was a caring friend. Although she had never experienced the death of a loved one, nor consoled someone who had, she knew Nancy was hurting. Just to be with her friend, Kris went over to Nancy's house. She was practicing the third rule of friendship: *Care for your friends.*

Carol Traub

Chapter 3

How to Know When It's Love

How does God fit into your dating?

Sixteen-year-old Jeff is deeply in love with Wendy. They live for the times they can be together, and right now nothing else seems to matter.

Is Jeff and Wendy's love the real thing? Of course! When they promise to love each other always, they really mean it. But we know that most people change in a lot of important ways between the ages of 15 and 21. Our values, our career and educational goals, and our attitudes are shaped and clarified as we observe the ways others live their lives.

Perspectives on love also evolve during this time. From one-sided "crushes" to mutual "love at first sight," we learn there are many different experiences of "love."

We love so many different things. Chocolate cake. Cats. Mountains. Football. Designer jeans. But there's something different about the love we discover when we love another person.

What makes this love different? How do we know it's true love? To answer that question, let's look at what love is and what it isn't.

► What Love Is

Only in the past 100 years have people tried to combine love, sex and marriage into "romantic love." Before that, people married for convenience or to rear families or to share work. Sometimes love developed for these couples, but not always. They didn't expect their partners to fulfill all their needs. Now we have enormous expectations. We want our mate to be a companion, a friend, a psychologist, a lover and someone to take out the garbage!

The biggest problem with the word "love" is that it covers so many feelings and expressions. Think about these examples:

- Odette would say she's "in love" because she has a major crush on the new center on the basketball team. She idolizes him, but she has never talked to him.
- Mark and Heidi "fell in love" at the youth group retreat last weekend. They'd never spent time together. Then they started talking at the retreat, and they've been in the clouds ever since.
- Mr. and Mrs. Alexander have been married 50 years. She had a stroke five years ago and

can't talk. Mr. Alexander says he'll always "love" her.

- Matthew and John have been best friends for several years. They'd probably never say they "love" each other, but they certainly care deeply about each other and enjoy being together.

Love might not be so confusing if we were like the ancient Greeks. While we just have one word for "love," they had three. These words tell us a lot about what love is:

- *Eros* means sexual love between two persons.
- *Philia* means the love between friends.
- *Agape* means God's love for people, or our selfless love for each other.

These definitions help us understand the differences among the kinds of love we experience. For example, we could say that Odette is in "eros" with the basketball star. Matthew and John share feelings of "philia." Mark and Heidi probably feel a mixture of "eros" and "philia" for each other. And Mr. and Mrs. Alexander are in "agape" with each other—though they probably feel "eros" and "philia" too.

► What Love Isn't

While these differences help us understand love, they don't tell us much about it. To learn more, let's look at what love isn't.

Consider some of today's common "love myths":

- **Myth #1:** ***If we are truly in love***

now, it will last a lifetime. Our high divorce rate illustrates the sad truth. Though love may seem strong, it's complicated and fragile as well. Love can die if it isn't carefully protected and nurtured.

• **Myth #2:** ***Real love means we'll never argue or disagree.*** Nonsense! For two people to hold identical interests, values and opinions, they'd have to be cloned. How boring! The important thing to remember is that differences can and must be worked out as they occur.

• **Myth #3:** ***Young love is the best love. It's all downhill after about age 25.*** Genuine love requires maturity. Teenage years are necessarily a time of self-centeredness and "trying on" different personalities as you seek emotional and financial independence from your parents. Many teenage marriages fall apart shortly after the honeymoon because of these factors.

• **Myth #4:** ***In God's plan for my life, there's only one particular person just for me.*** It is true, of course, that God loves and cares about us, and that we should seek his guidance in all our decisions. However, we shouldn't oversimplify this relationship by seeing him as a heavenly matchmaker! Remember, there are many people with whom you might find a good and true love, but there's no one perfect girl or guy just around the corner!

► How to Know the Difference

Now, let's assume for a moment that you have survived a couple of crushes, been teased about "puppy love," and fallen in and out of love a few times. You may have been burned by some unhappy and disastrous relationships. Or maybe you haven't dated yet. How will you know real love when it comes along?

Let's take a look at some practical guidelines for being able to recognize real love. Give your relationship a quick check by answering the following questions about these love statements:

- ***We're not afraid to question our feelings.*** Why have I chosen this person? Is the attraction mostly physical, or are we also friends? Can we spend significant periods of time together without "making out"?

- ***We respect and trust each other.*** Can each of us rejoice at the other person's success without feeling jealous? Do I feel I've never been taken advantage of for any reason? Am I allowed the private time and space I need to develop as an individual? Am I continuing to grow as a person? Can I share my deepest thoughts and know they'll be respected and kept confidential?

- ***We accept each other pretty much as we are.*** Can we each pursue separate interests without being harassed? Are we careful to avoid making our commitment to one another on feelings alone, knowing that emotional highs and lows are a common part of life?

- ***Sometimes each of us gives more than***

we get; we don't keep score. Does our love bring a strong desire to make the other person happy? to protect his or her interest? After the original intense, exciting feelings begin to subside, will we still seek and want the best for the other, while asking for our own fulfillment as well?

● ***Our love for each other has brought out the best in us.*** Are we becoming more kind and helpful toward members of our own families? Are we more responsible at school and/or work? Has our self-confidence bloomed in social situations? Are we both aware that God uses healthy relationships to bring order to our lives and honor to him?

► Is It True Love?

So, how can you know if it's really love? When all is said and done, there's no absolute, foolproof test.

But there is one good guide. First Corinthians 13 gives us a crystal-clear yardstick for measuring love. Evaluate your relationship based on the qualities listed in that important scripture passage. Insert your friend's name in the blanks:

	Always	Sometimes	Never
1. I am patient and kind with __________.	☐	☐	☐
2. I am not jealous or envious of __________.	☐	☐	☐
3. I am not boastful or proud with __________.	☐	☐	☐
4. I am not selfish or rude to __________.	☐	☐	☐
5. I am not irritable with __________.	☐	☐	☐
6. I don't hold grudges against __________.	☐	☐	☐
7. I am loyal to __________.	☐	☐	☐
8. I believe in __________, always expecting the best.	☐	☐	☐

How did you do? If you're like most people, you probably have a mixture of "Always," "Sometimes" and "Never." But if you find that you have more "Nevers" than anything else, you probably need to wait for and work toward true "agape" love. It's not something you get when you "fall in love." It's something you develop as you get to know, trust and respect each other.

Love is a tall order. But who can deny Paul's declaration: "These three remain: faith, hope, and love; and the greatest of these is love."

Barbara Nelson

Building a Relationship Before Marriage

Suppose you're dating someone. You think you have a great relationship. You enjoy doing everything together. You think you might even want to get married. Should you or shouldn't you?

Before you make any decisions, work on your relationship. Strong relationships help build strong marriages. Give your relationship time to grow and develop. Build a strong relationship—and possible marriage—by saying "I will" to the following tips.

- ***Get to know yourself first.*** Do you like yourself? Do you feel confident in what you value and believe? You need to feel good about yourself before you can feel good about accepting someone else's values and beliefs. "Tom and I don't agree on everything, but we respect each other's values and beliefs," says Kristy. "We support each other and love each other. And that's what matters."
- ***Practice open communication.*** Learn how to express your feelings as well as your ideas and needs. An open, trusting relationship allows both of you to be who you are—people with strengths and weaknesses. And an open, trusting relationship gives you a safe place to talk about your feelings—both positive and negative. "Not only is Jason my husband, he's also my best friend," says Tammi. "He listens to me. He cares about me."
- ***Have realistic expectations.*** Don't expect an A+ from your partner on every item on your list. If you think your partner has to be perfect, what will you do when he or she can't live up to your expectations? "Melanie doesn't think our marriage will work," says Brad after his first week of marriage. "She idolized me until she found out that I couldn't balance the checkbook or fix a leaking faucet. What does she expect? I'm not perfect."

Take time to get to know yourself. Develop a strong relationship. Practice open communication. Have realistic expectations. And remember, long-term relationships don't happen overnight.

Chapter 4

Sex: Why Wait?

How does God fit with your sexuality?

Shari and Robert were tense. They wanted to talk about their sexual relationship. They'd been dating for eight months. And they'd been going all the way for the past two months.

"I love Robert," Shari said. "I plan on marrying him in a few years. But we've got to stop having sex. It's bad, dirty and ugly. God says sex is wrong until after you're married."

Robert sighed. I could tell he was frustrated. "I think God's the great killjoy when it comes to sex," he said. "We aren't hurting anyone. We love each other. Shari's just making excuses."

I didn't know what to say. I disagree with Robert. God isn't the great killjoy when it comes to sex.

But I don't agree with Shari either. She believes God looks down on sex. It's true God wants you to wait until after marriage to have sex. But I believe he wants you to wait for good reasons.

I wish I could say I solved Robert and Shari's problem. That they stopped having sex until after they married. That they're now missionaries in Africa.

But I can't. Two weeks after we talked, they broke up. Shari's surviving. Robert hasn't shown up at church since.

► Evaluate Others' Opinions

Is Robert right? Is God the great killjoy when it comes to sex? I don't think so. But I didn't know how to say: "Yes, God wants you to wait until after marriage to have sex. But, no, he's not the great killjoy."

Or is Shari right? Throughout our conversation, she made sex sound dirty and ugly. And like God hates it. I appreciate Shari's desire to please God. But her opinion seems warped.

Shari should forget what she thinks the Bible says about sex. Why? Because someone taught her the wrong things. Well-meaning teachers told her sex is dirty, rotten and ugly, and that she should save this dirty, rotten, ugly experience for marriage.

But that isn't true. God doesn't see sexuality as dirty, rotten or ugly.

► Understand Sexuality

When God made us, he created our sexuality. In Genesis 2:18-25, God created Eve as Adam's partner. The only companions Adam had before

Eve were beasts and birds. They made great pets. But they weren't what Adam had in mind for a lifelong partner.

When Adam met Eve, he was excited. Genesis 2:24-25 describes their relationship as "a man leaves his father and mother and is united with his wife, and they become one. The man and the woman were both naked, but they were not embarrassed."

God created man and woman. He also created our bodies, minds and spirits. His hands made every aspect of our being. God created our sexuality, and it's his special gift to us.

► Honor God With Your Body

In 1 Corinthians 6:18-20, Paul says: "Flee from sexual immorality. All other sins a man commits are outside his body, but he who sins sexually sins against his own body. Do you not know that your body is a temple of the Holy Spirit, who is in you, whom you have received from God? You are not your own; you were bought at a price. Therefore honor God with your body."

A few points jump out of this passage. First, the body is God's temple. The Holy Spirit actually dwells in everyone's body. That means our bodies are special. And they should be treated with respect and honor. This applies to our sexuality, our eating habits and our physical condition.

This passage also says to glorify God with our bodies. We control what we do with our bodies. We can choose to honor God or dishonor God. Our decision about premarital sex may or may

How Far Is Too Far?

Touch is a natural way to express our feelings to a person of the opposite sex. But how much touch is okay? We know the Bible warns against sexual intercourse outside of marriage, but what about necking? or petting?

Nowhere in the Bible can we find "Thou shalt not engage in French kissing" or "Petting is an abomination." But the Bible is explicit on a related issue: lust. Jesus said, "Anyone who looks at a woman lustfully has already committed adultery with her in his heart" (Matthew 5:28).

Lust isn't simply our sexual appetite. Lust is that runaway desire that causes us to imagine having sexual intercourse with a person.

So it's okay to look at a person and say to yourself, "There's an attractive person." But if we think, "Hey, I wonder how that person is in bed," then we've stepped out of bounds.

Lust, then, provides some answers to the question, "How far is too far?" We've definitely gone too far if lust enters our minds.

Take a look at the "Lust Meter." You know yourself well. At what point on the meter will lustful thoughts enter your mind? In making contact with another person, at what point will thoughts of sexual intercourse race across your imagination? That point is definitely "too far" for you. You've entered a

continued

realm God considers as serious as any sex act you could commit.

Other people may identify a different level on the "Lust Meter" as the point where their lustful thoughts emerge. For example, psychologists say that males are usually sexually aroused before females.

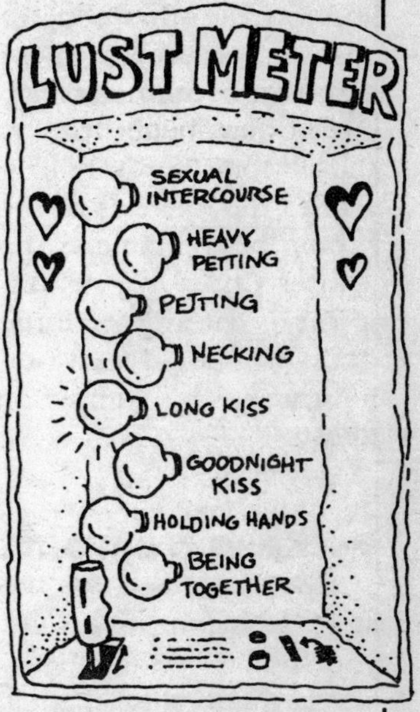

These differences raise another important issue. Romans 14:21 cautions us to do nothing that will cause others to fall into sin. So in a dating relationship each person should avoid doing anything that could cause the other person to lust. While your "too far" point on the meter may not be at lustful thoughts, your date's "too far" point might be.

How do you know your date's "too far" point? Talk about it. That's difficult to do. But your openness will be a sign of maturity. Real relationships require communication—especially on sensitive subjects.

Thom Schultz

not honor our Lord.

God asks us to honor him with our bodies—and to treat other people with care. In Philippians 2:3-5, Paul says: "Do nothing out of selfish ambition or vain conceit, but in humility consider others better than yourselves. Each of you should look not only to your own interests, but also to the interests of others. Your attitude should be the same as that of Christ Jesus."

Jesus Christ lives within the people we date. And our dates deserve the same respect as Jesus does. We should treat our dates respectfully, taking care not to trample on their concerns and interests.

► Keep From Sinning

What does God say about premarital sex? Look at 1 Thessalonians 4:3-4: "It is God's will that you should be sanctified: that you should avoid sexual immorality; that each of you should learn to control his own body in a way that is holy and honorable."

The Greek word for immorality in this passage can also be translated as fornication. And that means "unmarried people having sex." The Bible clearly says God wants us to avoid premarital sex. And he wants us to honor him with our bodies.

I believe everyone should wait until after they get married to have sex. But not everyone may agree. Some teenagers say they love each other. They say they plan to get married anyway.

That's the wrong reason to go all the way. Some studies show the average person falls in love with five different people between ninth grade and the second year of college. Just because a couple falls in love doesn't mean the two will eventually marry. Most high school "loves" don't last past graduation.

C.S. Lewis, in his book *The Screwtape Letters*, says whenever a man lies with a woman, a powerful relationship forms. And both must either enjoy—or endure—the relationship forever. Too many teenagers don't choose self-control. So they end up living with their mistakes forever.

► How to Say No

Teenagers have sex for a lot of reasons. They say it makes them more intimate and less lonely. They feel afraid the relationship would fall apart. They feel bored. They say everybody else does it.

But the #1 reason teenagers say they have sex is because they can't say no. Sometimes it's hard to say no. But you can avoid having sex by saying no these ways:

- Shake your head.
- Say you don't feel like it.
- Find other, creative ways to show you love each other, such as making dinner for each other, singing duets, writing poetry or hiding notes of appreciation in each other's locker.
- Say you'd rather wait.
- Say that sex before marriage is dumb.
- Make your standards clear before the relationship gets too steamy.
- Say you're not ready for sex yet and to check back in a few years.

- Say you're not that kind of person.
- Say if the person loves you, he or she will understand and not pressure you to do something you don't want to do.
- Avoid tempting situations.
- Say no, and mean it.

► Wait Until Marriage

It's clear God says to wait until after marriage to have sex. It's also clear that God wants us to have the best.

Is it easy to wait until after marriage to have sex? Not always.

Is it best? Yes.

Jim Burns

Chapter 5

Dollars and Sense

How does God fit into your money matters?

Allison stares at the black sneakers in the special shoe-store display at the mall. She glances down at the white ones on her feet. They still look new. She bought them two months ago.

But black sneakers—not white ones—are in right now. Allison wonders what to do. She doesn't have enough money. But she doesn't want to go to school wearing out-of-style shoes.

Allison pulls out her credit card. She has to have those shoes.

On the other side of the mall, Brian looks at car accessories. Last week he finished redoing his car's interior. Now he's thinking of adding a few racing stripes to the body. He wants his car to look spectacular. And when it does, he'll ask Allison out to a movie.

Spending money is easy. But using it wisely isn't. Look at how you spend your money. What does it say about you?

► What Does Jesus Think?

Jesus never bought sneakers. He never wore designer jeans. And he never owned a car or a house. But he did say a lot about money.

- **Don't let money become #1.** In Matthew 6:24-34, Jesus makes it clear that God should come first. Even people who don't have much can put things first by constantly worrying about them.
- **Use your money wisely.** Jesus doesn't want you to waste your money. In the parable of the talents in Matthew 25:14-30, the master blessed the two servants who doubled the money he gave them. Another servant blew it. He hid his money in the ground.
- **Give your money to the poor.** Throughout the New Testament, Jesus identifies with the hungry and homeless. He even tells the rich man in Mark 10:17-31 the way to get eternal life: Sell everything and give all the money to the poor.

► What Do Others Think?

Many teenagers think money means success. Most teenage guys define success as having money and wealth. They dread the thought of unemployment.

"We want fancy cars, spending money, all the luxuries of being rich," says a 15-year-old from Kansas. This teenager and others who are success-minded attend summer camps to learn how to manage mutual funds.

These camps aren't like Bible camp. And they aren't cheap. Dollars & Cents camp in Marco Is-

Your Wheel of Fortune

Spin through these wheel of fortune statements. Circle true or false. Then look at the answers (on page 55).

1. As a whole, teenagers spend more than $40 billion of their families' budget each year. True/False

2. Most teenagers get money from their parents. True/False

3. Guys spend more money on cars and gasoline than anything else. True/False

4. Most teenagers have their own savings accounts. Few have checking accounts. True/False

5. The average allowance for a 16-year-old American is $9.13 a week. True/False

6. Most teenagers think their families buy more than they need. True/False

7. Girls rate shopping their #1 pastime. They enjoy it more than dating. True/False

8. Most teenagers use credit cards. True/False

land, Florida, and Young Americans Success Camp in Midway, Utah, cost up to $1,450 a week.

► What's Wrong With That?

Money can be dangerous. It can threaten your relationship with God. It can trick you into looking only at yourself. And it can make you greedy.

"Frankly, I'm convinced the world doesn't take [Christians] seriously because we're so much like the world," author Tom Sine says. "We're caught up in the same miserable rat race of self-seeking consumerism and materialism."

Not all teenagers are caught up in that rat race. Some teenagers don't have any money. They live with families that can't afford food or clothing.

In El Salvador, most of the nation's population is 15 or younger. More than half the teenagers can't find jobs or are underemployed. Many don't know what to do. Their future looks bleak.

In other countries, children never get the chance to become teenagers. About 40,000 children die every day from starvation and malnutrition.

► How Can You Respond?

What can you do? A lot. Experts estimate $100 will save one starving child's life. If U.S. citizens gave the money they spend on soft drinks every year to the poor, about 230 million hungry children could be saved.

Does that mean you should stop drinking soft drinks? Not necessarily. But this example illustrates how you can cut down on some of the luxuries you don't need. And you can get more satisfaction while using your money wisely and sharing it with the needy.

Begin by looking in your drawers and closets. Take an inventory of your wardrobe. Do you really need to buy the most fashionable outfit when the one you bought six months ago still looks good? How can you justify that when other teenagers in this world don't have any choice of what to wear?

Then evaluate your budget. Don't spend money as soon as you get it. Begin making decisions

Your Wheel of Fortune Answers

1. True. Younger teenagers (ages 12-15) spend an average of about $20 per week, but older teenagers (ages 16-17) spend $31 per week.
2. True. About 40 percent of teenagers get money from their parents when they ask; and 29 percent get regular allowances. Only 33 percent have regular jobs.
3. False. Guys spend more money on movies, dating and entertainment than anything else.
4. True. About 74 percent of teenagers have their own savings accounts. Only 17 percent have checking accounts.
5. False. The average 16-year-old gets $8.13 a week for allowance.
6. True. About 54 percent of teenagers agree that their families buy more than they need.
7. True. Of 100,000 girls surveyed, 93 percent say they enjoy shopping best. They rate boys and dating sixth on their list of favorite activities.
8. False. Only 12 percent of teenagers use credit cards.

Getting a Handle on Your Money

Most likely you get money every month. You may work for it. Or you may get an allowance.

Before you spend your money, think ahead. You can stretch your dollars just by planning. Fill in this chart. Start by writing your monthly income. Then set aside money for tithing and savings. See what you can buy with the rest. Just make sure your monthly income is greater than or equal to your total expenses.

Your monthly income: $ ____________

Your monthly expenses:

Church, charities	$ ____________
Savings	$ ____________
Clothes	$ ____________
Movies, entertainment	$ ____________
Car, transportation	$ ____________
Food, snacks	$ ____________
Hobbies	$ ____________
Miscellaneous	$ ____________

Total $ ____________

about how to use money. Put some in the bank. Give some to the poor. Don't spend it all on yourself.

And begin to see your money as God's money. God gives you everything. Your money belongs to God. Think of it this way: Don't ask how much money you should give to God. Instead, ask how much of God's money you should keep.

Jesus' message about money is clear. He wants you to put God first in your life. He wants you to use your money wisely. And he wants you to help the poor.

That may not seem easy. But when you use God's gifts wisely, you'll discover sneakers and racing stripes don't bring true happiness.

Giving and loving do.

Jolene L. Roehlkepartain

Chapter 6

Surviving School Stress

How does God fit into your school life?

What's the most nerve-racking part of school? If you're like most teenagers, you'll probably say, when you get your report card. Or the day of final exams. Or anything else related to grades.

In fact, what most teenagers wish they could change about themselves is getting better grades. And 82 percent of teenagers will tell you that schoolwork worries them.

Adults understand these school pressures. High school principal Bob Poirier surveyed his school's freshmen to find out their needs. The #1 response? Help in dealing with stress. And Poirier believes a major source of that stress comes from grades.

Teenagers agree. Liana, 16, says grades are her

biggest worry. And while John, 17, feels that making and keeping friends are his top priorities, grades follow close behind.

► The Stress Express

Why do grades cause so much stress? Many teenagers feel grades judge a person's self-worth. Teenagers who make the honor roll often get their names published in the community newspaper. Schools often recognize students who graduate with distinction. Yet most people in education will say grades have a positive purpose.

High school teacher Ron Garofalo believes grades are nothing more than a measure of performance. "If there wasn't such a thing as grades," he says, "you'd have very little accountability or motivation to do well."

And for many teenagers, grades do motivate. "I want to excel. I don't want to just sit back and do poorly when I know I can do a lot better."

But people often overemphasize grades. Colleges rely on grades in the admissions process. And that can be unfair. "At 15, you may be going through family problems, and you may blow your grades all sophomore year," Poirier says. "You can say, 'Why am I going to be held accountable for that when I get to college, law school or medical school?' "

Colleges are getting better. In the last few years, school counselors have noticed colleges becoming more realistic. Some colleges realize good students are more well-rounded and may not get top grades. They go after B students

Getting Great Grades

Did your last report card make you shudder? Do you want to do better in school? Would you like to get higher grades? Try these suggestions to improve your grades.

- **Go to class.** Missing the day's lesson means missing important information. Absenteeism and tardiness often lower your grades.

- **Study.** Students making mostly A's report studying about two hours above the average per week, while students making mostly D's say they study about four hours less than the average.

- **Find a study partner.** It's easier to motivate yourself to study if someone else is there with you. Choose a study partner who will really help you and will always be on time.

- **Begin class projects and reports as soon as they're assigned.** Plan your schoolwork. Most kids wait until one or two days before the project is due before they start working on it, then grumble when their grades aren't good.

- **Turn off the television.** If you're a TV junkie, cut down the number of hours you spend watching it. For example, instead of watching four shows a night, select only the one you "just can't miss." Use the rest of your evening to study, read and talk with family members.

- **Get God involved.** Study hard, then ask God to help you with mental recall, concentration and a clear mind during the test. Ask God to help you stay motivated and dedicated.

Alan Maki

Test Your School IQ

We hear all kinds of rumors about public and private schools. "Private schools teach better values." "You can't get a good education at a public school."

What's true? What's not? For each of the following rumors, checkmark whether you think the statement is true or false. Turn to page 65 to see how you did.

Rumors	True	False
1. The dropout rate is higher in public schools.	______	______
2. Teenagers are more sexually active in public schools.	______	______
3. More teachers in private schools have graduate degrees.	______	______
4. More teenagers in private schools believe God is interested in their sexual behavior.	______	______
5. A greater percentage of teenagers in private schools attend a four-year college after graduation.	______	______

who're involved in many activities, not just straight-A students who study all the time.

But colleges still need to make changes. And so do parents. When they overemphasize grades, their expectations add to the stress. And although too much pressure isn't good, no pressure at all isn't good either.

► Your Stress Report Card

No matter what colleges and parents think, the pressure to do well will always be around. How can you deal with that pressure?

Grade yourself on how well you cope with these stressful situations. Give yourself an A if the situation doesn't cause you any stress. Or an F if the situation makes you completely stressed-out. Give yourself B's, C's and D's for the various degrees of stress between A's and F's.

1. Your math teacher throws a pop quiz. You're two days behind in your studies. ________
2. Tomorrow you're scheduled to give a speech about AIDS. You just can't get started. It's already midnight, and you still haven't written anything. ________
3. You hurry home from school to check the mailbox for your report card. But your dad got home early and has already seen it. ________
4. You need to get an A in history to make the honor roll. You get a test back with a C- on it. ________
5. It's finals week. All six of your

teachers scheduled final exams on the same day. ________

► Less-Stress Steps

How did you do? Were you honest with yourself? Or did you feel pressured to give yourself all A's? Did you give yourself grades higher than you should have? If so, you probably feel pressured to always make the best grades.

What steps can you take to keep your pressures in perspective? Try these suggestions:

- **Keep up with your schoolwork.** If you do assignments as soon as you get them, great! If not, set up a regular study schedule. Then stick to it.
- **Focus on learning, not grades.** John and Liana tackle their assignments honestly. They do more than finding one textbook answer. "If I feel I've studied hard enough," Liana says, "I don't worry about what the test score says."
- **Ask for help.** When you don't understand something, ask your teacher. Or ask all your teachers about areas you need to improve. "That tells me what I need to work on," Liana says, "instead of just having a grade."
- **Tell the truth.** If there's a reason for your poor performance, let your teacher know. Many teachers are understanding. "If a student goes to a teacher and says, 'My sister attempted suicide last night,' the teacher will make adjustments in the academic workload for that student," Poirier says.
- **Talk with your parents.** Find out what

The School Scoop

Rumors can distort the truth. Here's the straight school scoop to the quiz on page 62:

1. True. According to a USA Today poll, 14 percent of public school students drop out, compared with 11 percent of private school students.

2. False. Twenty percent more private school students than public school students are sexually active, according to the Loomis Institute.

3. False. The U.S. Department of Education reports that 52 percent of public school teachers have a master's or a doctorate degree compared with 31 percent of private school teachers.

4. False. Religion seems to affect the values of public high school students more than private school students, according to a study in Adolescence journal.

5. True. According to a University of Chicago sociologist, private Catholic school graduates are 10 percent more likely to go to college than public school graduates.

Jolene L. Roehlkepartain

Survival Gear for School

Looking sharp on your first day of school is important. But you also need to survive. Now you can do both by wearing an outfit designed to be durable and fashionable.

Radio Shack firefighter's helmet—This helmet, which you can borrow from your little brother, will keep you from being stepped on by 7-foot-2-inch seniors.

Gas mask—This mask will help your nose adjust to the ecological ambiance (smelly air) of gym locker rooms.

Life preserver—When that sinking feeling hits you on your first day, a life preserver will keep you floating.

Compass—To find your way through the halls and/or avoid the cafeteria, use a compass.

Air Force flight suit—This suit has lots of pockets for maps (of school); Rolaids; Pepto-Bismol; extra food; matches and firewood (for when you're lost in the halls); and miscellaneous first-aid items.

Parachute—For those times when you feel like bailing out, a parachute is your best resort.

Airline airsickness bag—Bring this to lunch. You'll know why you need it.

Kneepads—Kneepads will keep your knees from chafing after a day of constantly dropping to the ground for prayer.

Backpack—A backpack will hold your first day's assignments from first period class. Empty it between classes. Sublet additional locker space from upperclassmen if necessary.

Swim fins—For times when you want to keep your head above water, use swim fins.

J. Brent Bill

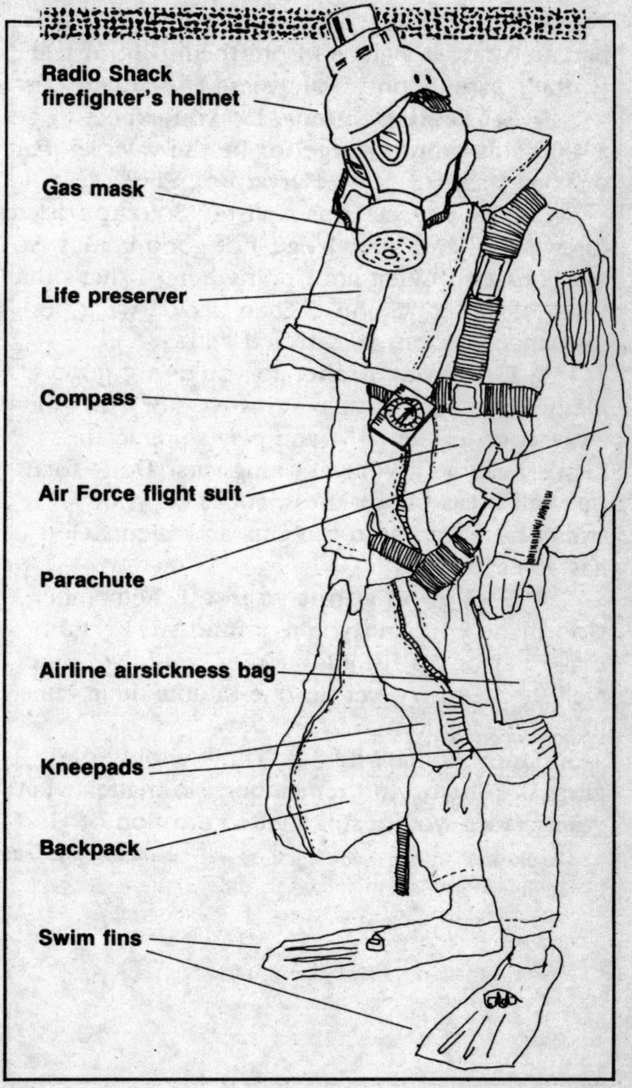
Radio Shack
firefighter's helmet
Gas mask
Life preserver
Compass
Air Force flight suit
Parachute
Airline airsickness bag
Kneepads
Backpack
Swim fins

your parents expect. Some teenagers think their parents want straight A's from them. But in reality, their parents only want them to do their best.

● **Set realistic goals.** Do you expect to get a 4.0 grade-point average? or be the valedictorian of your class? or go to Harvard or Yale?

Are those expectations realistic? Solomon asked for wisdom and knowledge, not good grades. So ask yourself: "What am I doing here? What's the value of my education?" Then decide what performance you can be satisfied with.

● **Find your niche.** So you're not good at math. Have you written a creative story that blew away your teacher? Do you play solos in the band? Are you a whiz at fixing cars? Don't focus on your areas of weakness. Focus on your strengths. Take joy in the gifts and talents God has given you.

● **Feel good about yourself.** Remember: God made you, and you're important. I doubt that Peter or his fishing buddies would've done well in chemistry, yet no one doubts their value in God's kingdom.

So study Romans 12:3-8. Think about your gifts. Use them. And remember: No matter what your grades, you're still a gifted creation of God.

Karen Fisber

Chapter 7

Listen to the Music

How does God fit into your music choices?

Rock 'n' roll, like all music, has a message. That message may be love or hate, peace or war, drugs or faith, but there's always a message. It may be funny, heavy, sad or ridiculous. But it's there. And we may not notice it as it pounds away in the background. But it's there.

Try this experiment: Ask some friends which songs they like best. When they tell you, ask them what they like about the songs.

If they're like most people, it won't be the lyrics that attract them. In fact, if you ask them what the words say, they'll probably think about it a while or just reply, "I dunno."

The beat goes on, and so do the lyrics. They're always perched somewhere in the back of our minds waiting to fly through our heads. Those messages affect us, even though we may not be conscious of them.

The Sounds of Scripture

If you're searching for direction when it comes to rock music, dig into God's Word. Find out what God says about life, music and your choices. Read each Bible passage, and next to each one write what God is telling you.

Bible passage	**What God is telling me**
Deuteronomy 6:5-9	______________________
	______________________
Psalm 150	______________________
	______________________
Romans 12:1-2, 9	______________________
	______________________
Galatians 5:19-25	______________________
	______________________
Ephesians 5:1-2, 19	______________________
	______________________
Philippians 4:8	______________________
	______________________
Colossians 3:16-17	______________________
	______________________

► Sound Listening

How do you decide whether the music you're listening to is good for you? As a responsible Christian, it's important to be a careful listener. Here's how:

- **Listen to the beat and melody.** What's your strongest feeling when you listen to the song? Do you feel happy? lonely? violent? depressed? hopeful? other? Would you rather be alone or with others when you listen to the song?
- **Observe the performers and singers.** What are their "best value" songs about? What are their "worst value" songs about?
- **Catch the words of each song.** What real-life issue is the song about? Is the song suggesting you do something about its issue? For example, have sex? feed the hungry? use drugs? protest nuclear war? Could you talk with your parents about the song's issue?
- **Compare your musical taste with your friends'.** Have you ever said you liked a song or rock group just because your friends said they did? Do you secretly listen to one kind of music while publicly acting like you listen to what your friends like?

► Sound Choices

Being a selective listener means that you are careful about what you listen to. Song titles often give a clue to what's coming on. After all, when you hear "Harry the Hairy Ape" you can be pretty sure it's not about making out in the back seat of a Buick. But when you hear "If lovin' you is

Favorite Musicians Interviews

Imagine you're assigned to interview a musician—a secular rock singer, a contemporary Christian artist, a country singer or a heavy metal band leader. Choose who you'd interview, and jot down what you'd ask and tell that person.

Musician's name:

One question I'd like to ask this musician is:

One thing I'd like to tell this musician is:

Who's Your Favorite?

Answer these questions and share your responses with a friend.

1. Who's your favorite musical performer (Christian or secular)?

2. Describe how you feel about that performer's . . .
   lyrics:

   sound and style of music:

   looks and dress:

   personality:

   lifestyle:

3. Read Philippians 4:8: "Fill your minds with those things that are good and that deserve praise: things that are true, noble, right, pure, lovely, and honorable."

4. Does your favorite group "measure up" to these standards? Why or why not?

5. Does God play into your decision about a favorite performer? Why or why not?

A Music Crossword Puzzle

How well do you know music? As you solve this crossword puzzle, watch out for the following puzzlers.

Across

1. To sing with your lips closed.
3. A small, stringed instrument in Daniel 3:10.
5. Words to a song.
6. A long-playing record with many songs.
9. A device to muffle an instrument's sound.
10. The lowest, basic note of a musical scale.
11. A reed instrument often used in jazz.
12. An album that has sold one million copies.

continued

Across (con't.)

16. Annual music award.
18. Speaker that reproduces high-frequencies.
19. The musicians in 2 Chronicles 5:11-14.
21. Jazz developed between 1945 and 1955.
22. Another word for a duet.
25. Recording played on laser beam device.
26. Abbreviation for Digital Audio Tapes.
27. A collection of music from a motion picture.
29. A group of three voices or three instruments.
31. The highest singing voice in a four-part choir.
32. Heavy metal band that quotes Isaiah 53:5.
33. Means "may it be so."
34. A person who sells concert tickets illegally.

Down

1. Songs Christians sing (see Colossians 3:16).
2. The queen of soul; ___________ Franklin.
3. An old instrument related to the guitar.
4. An abbreviation for frequency modulation.
6. A well-known contemporary Christian artist.
7. The first instrument Tracy Chapman played.
8. Syllable for the fifth tone of a singing scale.
9. Magazine for heavy metal music lovers.
13. Strings on David's harp (Psalm 144:9).
14. The main tune of a song; the leading part.
15. A Hebrew music term (Psalm 68:32).
16. Where Elvis Presley fans flock to pay tribute.
17. A TV station that plays music videos.
18. The instrument Miriam played in Exodus 15.
20. The director of an orchestra.
23. An amusement park in Nashville, Tennessee.
24. The speaker that reproduces low-frequencies.
25. Music Mozart and Bach wrote.
28. The lowest range for a male singer.
30. An instrument usually found in churches.

Jolene L. Roehlkepartain

wrong, I don't want to be right," you can be just as sure that it's not going to have a Christian Housekeeping seal of approval.

So pay attention to the clues—don't buy into songs just because they sound nice or pretty. Don't be sucked in by a driving beat.

Paying attention takes work. Spend a few minutes now playing an album (or tune in your favorite station). Listen *carefully.* Do you hear what's being said? Do you agree with it? If not, how are you going to respond to that song now?

► Sound Advice

When you hear a song that has a terrible message, have the courage to change the station. That's right—*courage.* Because as soon as you change the station, a friend will yelp: "Why'd you change that? That's my favorite song!" So you're either going to have to change it back or explain why you changed it. To be a selective listener means that you may face some ridicule from your friends. But anything worth believing is worth standing up for.

J. Brent Bill

Answers

Across: 1. Hum. 3. Lyre. 5. Lyrics. 6. Album. 9. Mute. 10. Keynote. 11. Saxophone. 12. Platinum. 16. Grammy. 18. Tweeter. 19. Levites. 21. Bop. 22. Duo. 25. CD. 26. DAT. 27. Soundtrack. 29. Trio. 31. Soprano. 32. Stryper. 33. Amen. 34. Scalper.

Down: 1. Hymns. 2. Aretha. 3. Lute. 4. FM. 6. Amy. 7. Ukulele. 8. Sol. 9. Metallix. 13. Ten. 14. Melody. 15. Selah. 16. Graceland. 17. MTV. 18. Tambourine. 20. Conductor. 23. Opryland. 24. Woofer. 25. Classical. 28. Bass. 30. Organ.

Chapter 8

Working Part Time: Is It Worth It?

How does God fit into your job?

The extra money sounds great. And you think the experience would be good. Sure, busing tables on the fast-food strip isn't the greatest way to spend your Saturdays. But at least it earns a little extra money for clothes, gas and entertainment.

If you decide to take the job, you're not unusual. There are enough working teenagers to staff almost 250,000 McDonald's—35 times the number of McDonald's that exist in the world today. And most teenagers with jobs work in places like McDonald's. They work in fast-food, retail and other service jobs—what a Harvard professor calls "McJobs."

Teenagers generally feel enthusiastic about their jobs. But some experts aren't sure they should be. They worry that teenagers who spend too many hours flipping burgers or sacking groceries end up with overloaded schedules and lower grades.

► Who Works?

Mixing school and work hasn't always been a problem. Forty years ago only a quarter of 16- and 17-year-old males worked. But today eight out of 10 teenagers will juggle school and work before they graduate.

Experts explain that the recent growth of the service and retail industries caused the shift. Shopping malls and hamburger joints need workers who don't mind small paychecks and odd hours. And teenagers fit that description perfectly.

► Why Worry?

So what's the problem? A teenager gets a little extra spending money. And a business makes bigger profits. Doesn't everyone benefit?

Psychologists Ellen Greenberger and Laurence Steinberg don't look at it that way. They wrote *When Teenagers Work* to argue that work and school don't mix. They go so far as to say, "The more time kids work, the worse off they are." Here's why:

- **Many teenagers are already too busy.** Adding 20 hours of work to an already busy schedule quickly adds up. "We have students putting in 70- or 80-hour weeks between school and work," worries Lou Kubler, a high school teacher in Florida. That doesn't leave much time for other activities.

Does Your Work Interfere?

What about you? Does working interfere with other areas of your life? Take this short self-test to find out.

	Always	Sometimes	Never
1. I plan all my other activities around my work schedule.	☐	☐	☐
2. My parents nag me about not getting things done around the house because I'm always working.	☐	☐	☐
3. My schoolwork suffers because I work (incomplete assignments, lower grades).	☐	☐	☐
4. I don't have time to participate in the extracurricular activities I want to do.	☐	☐	☐
5. My friends say things like, "We never get to see you now that you're working."	☐	☐	☐

Now, add up your score using this formula for each of the previous statements:

Always: 4 points
Sometimes: 2 points
Never: 0 points
Your total: ____________________

- If you scored higher than 15, re-evaluate your work. It's interfering with other areas of your life.
- If you scored between 10 and 15, you're in a danger zone. Find ways to cut your workload.
- If you scored between 5 and 10, you're probably doing okay. But keep an eye on your work so the load doesn't get heavier.
- If you scored less than 5, congratulations! You've found a way to balance your work and the rest of your life.

Teenagers who work know that their jobs knock them out of other activities. Seventeen-year-old Laura Hamrick of North Carolina drives a bus before and after school. But since bands and clubs meet then, she can't participate like she used to—and wants to.

● **Grades suffer.** Students who work long hours don't do well in school, Greenberger says. As 17-year-old Kirby Ekwall of Texas says, "It's just easier to get through school when you don't work."

In fact, this concern is the main reason many teenagers don't work—or why their parents won't let them. Jeriel Caballero, a 15-year-old in Illinois, says she doesn't really want to work when she turns 16. She'd prefer to "concentrate on my studies."

● **Work interferes with church.** Because teenagers work mostly on weekends, jobs often conflict with church activities. Mark Jones, a youth minister in North Carolina, says that many teenagers who work miss youth group meetings and Sunday morning worship.

Melissa Hogston knows that well. She didn't like working Sundays at her cafeteria job. "I had to skip church or leave in the middle of the service," the 17-year-old from North Carolina explains. "And that really bothered me."

Dan Scherer sometimes has the same problem. On Sunday, if the 17-year-old from Washington has to open the pizza place where he works, he misses church. And if he has to close Sunday evening, he misses the youth group meeting.

Once Dan forgot to request time off for youth

Sunday at church. The morning before the youth Sunday, he realized he was supposed to be two places at once. "Saturday morning I went running around trying to get people to do the early shift," he remembers. "But people don't like opening, so I had a real hard time." Fortunately, he found someone in time and could help at church.

Melissa and Dan aren't the only teenagers whose work interferes at times. Almost 75 percent of high school seniors feel work meddles with their social lives, according to the Institute of Social Research, University of Michigan. And half say work interferes with their school and family life.

► Why Work?

Most teenagers know about these problems, but still find work enjoyable and beneficial. Of course, the most obvious benefit is the extra money. "I like to have my own money without having to ask my parents for it," says Terry Wheeler, 17, of Texas. Some teenagers like Terry use that money for car payments and gas. Others save it for college.

Teenagers who work also say their jobs teach them responsibility, give them skills, and introduce them to the "real world." "I'm learning how to keep a schedule and budget money," explains Charles Roush, 16, who works at a K mart in Missouri.

Tami Runyan agrees. She works at a California boutique. The 17-year-old says her job has taught

What to Look for in a Job

We asked teenagers what advice they'd give friends who are looking for jobs. Here are their suggestions:

"Find something you think you'd enjoy. Then find out what kind of schedule you could get that would fit in with your schedule."

Melissa Hogston, 17
Boiling Springs, North Carolina

"Find out how much they pay per hour. Ask how many hours they expect you to work. And find out how lenient they are on changing that schedule."

Charles Roush, 16
Kansas City, Missouri

"Make sure you still have time for yourself and your friends. And don't let anyone take advantage of you just because you're a teenager."

Marisa Anderson, 17
Sonoma, California

"In some jobs you've got to be faster, and in some jobs you've got to be more polite. So find a place to work that fits your skills and personality."

Terry Wheeler, 17
Waco, Texas

"Ask people where they work. If you're going to put in an application someplace, ask someone who works there about the job before you take it."

Brian Hof, 16
Grandview, Missouri

her how to run a store, which will help her sales career. And when she works, she's the only worker in the store. So she's in charge.

Melissa sees similar benefits. She no longer works in the cafeteria. And since she's thinking of becoming an accountant, she believes her new job in the Sears catalog department will help. "I'm getting a lot of training in computers and working with people," she says. "I feel like what I do right now is pretty good training for what I may do in the future."

Job Stress

With school, relationships, church and extracurricular activities, a job usually multiplies your stress. Here are tips to help make your job responsibilities manageable and enjoyable:

- **Evaluate your expectations.** Ask yourself, "What do I hope to gain as a result of working besides earning money?" Do you hope to gain new skills, make new friends, get experience in a particular field or work in an area that might help you make a vocational choice? Prioritize your reasons, and then look for a job that meets your top three priorities.
- **Broaden your perspective.** Look for new ways to view what you do. If you work in a food-providing job, think of what you do as more than making tacos or washing dishes. Rather, see your work as benefiting people by feeding them or cleaning up after them.
- **Go the extra mile.** If you see how your job helps people, it's easy to do more than they expect. Offer a helping hand, give someone a smile, compliment work well done.
- **Take care of your spiritual life.** No matter how much you need money, don't let a job separate you from Christian fellowship and worship. And spend personal time with God.
- **Help build the kingdom.** Your job can give you opportunities to share God's love. If you're honest, work hard and relate personably to staff and customers, you'll share your faith in a visible way with your co-workers and customers.
- **Take time for play.** Waking early for school, going directly to work after classes and returning home late at night to crash into bed is no way to live. Remember to make time to play.
- **Talk with your parents.** Your parents want you to learn the responsibilities that go along with holding a job, but not at the expense of unreasonable physical, emotional or spiritual stress. Talk with your parents about any job-related stresses you have. Let your parents be a source of ideas, support and comfort.

Dub Ambrose

► Why Not?

Some teenagers have found ways to avoid the traps that working sets. Since working long or late hours causes the most problems, many young people make special arrangements to avoid those traps.

For instance, Gregory Bohanan is looking for a job, but he doesn't want it to interfere with his schoolwork. So the 16-year-old from Illinois has applied to usher during concerts and football games. That way he'll work only on weekends, when he has the time. And since the job is only on Friday and Saturday nights, he won't have to juggle work and church activities.

► Should You Work?

As you can see, juggling school and work isn't always easy. Some people are better jugglers than others. Maybe you're a good juggler who can handle lots of activities. Or maybe you know working could hurt your grades.

Before you take that job on the fast-food strip, decide whether the benefits outweigh the disadvantages. Is the money worth the time? Will working now help you in the future? Or should you concentrate on school, church or other activities?

Think through the options. Then avoid the traps that experts worry about.

Eugene C. Roehlkepartain

Chapter 9

Wanting to Win

• •

How does God fit into your sports and recreation?

You're playing your best friend in a lively game of tennis. It's a tough match; you've split the first two sets. You desperately want to win the third set.

Is that wrong?

•

Your high school football team's opponent boasts the top receiver in the county, and you're assigned to cover him. He's been beating you all night. You decide you're going to try to injure him and put him out of the game. After all, he's keeping your team from winning, and you want to help your team.

Is that wrong?

•

Your high school basketball team is playing the best team in the league. The teams battle through two overtimes, but the other team pulls it out on a last-second basket. After the game, you're depressed.

Is that wrong?

•

Competition brings up many questions that aren't easy to answer. Is it wrong to enjoy winning? Is the "killer instinct" unchristian? Should Christians be able to shrug off losing as "God's will"? Every athlete who's been serious about his or her faith has struggled with these questions. How does competitiveness—the desire to win—mesh with Christianity?

► Competitiveness: Right or Wrong

Whether in school, sports, your faith or your future career, there's nothing wrong with wanting to do well. The desire to win isn't itself evil; neither is any other desire to succeed.

Some Christian teenagers have trouble accepting this. After all, aren't we supposed to give up everything for Christ? If we want something, doesn't that automatically mean it's bad? But the Bible doesn't teach that simply wanting something is wrong.

On the other hand, success isn't automatically right, either. I hate to contradict the great coach Vince Lombardi, but winning isn't everything. And it isn't the only thing either. When winning becomes a god, sports are harmful. So let's take a balanced look at competitiveness—the good and the bad. That way you can compete, enjoy it and grow from it.

► Competitiveness: Good

Why are competitiveness and sports good? Here are three important lessons they teach:

● ***The reward of working hard toward a goal.*** If you've ever been a part of a winning team, you know what I mean. It feels good to capture a championship after you've put a lot of work into it.

Faith is the same way. In 1 Corinthians 9:24, Paul compared the Christian life to a race: "Do you not know that in a race all the runners run, but only one gets the prize? Run in such a way as to get the prize."

● ***The importance of teamwork.*** Every team needs a variety of talents. A basketball team of all centers wouldn't get the ball up the court. In sports, each team member matters. Read 1 Corinthians 12:12-26. What applies to sports applies to church too.

You can even learn teamwork from individual sports. Can you explain how each part of your body contributes to the tennis serve? or the golf swing? I can't. All I know is that when all parts work together correctly the ball goes in the right direction.

● ***How to bounce back from adversity.*** I used to lead a Bible study for high school football players in Redlands, California. I hated to see them lose because I knew how hard they had worked and how important winning was to them. So every season, after the first loss, we'd study Philippians 3:13-14: "But one thing I do:

BEST

Forgetting what is behind and straining toward what is ahead, I press on."

Coaches are fond of the quote, "Losing is worse than death, because you have to live with losing." But the opposite is true: Losing is better, because you can't bounce back from death! Dealing with sports-related disappointments now will help you learn in life. You'll suffer failures. But if you overcome adversity, it'll make future bumps smoother.

► Competitiveness: Bad

In addition to these benefits, though, there's a negative side to competitiveness. By recognizing the dangers, you can deal with them. Here are a few:

- ***Hating your opponent.*** One misconception in sports is that you have to hate your opponent to win. It's not true. Your main competition isn't your opponent; it's you. As a writer commented in Current Health magazine: "The challenge isn't to be the best. It's to do your best."

Think about it: Would God want you to participate in sports if you'd have to hate people?

Next time you're in an athletic contest, don't look at your opponents as people who are keeping you from reaching a goal or trying to take something you want (victory). Look at them as people who give you the opportunity to do your best, and as people you can help do the same.

- ***Associating personal worth with winning and losing.*** There's nothing wrong with feeling bad about losing. But it's easy to take that too far and tie your self-image to the scoreboard. After all, there's so much pressure—from coaches, classmates and even parents—that it's easy to feel worthless when you lose.

If winning is so important, you can always find people to beat. You could find plenty of beginners to drag onto the tennis court and whip. But that's not the reason to compete. As James Michener wrote in his book *Sports in America*, "Losing 6-3, 6-2 to a fine player is more rewarding than beating some beginner 6-0, 6-0."

• ***Losing perspective.*** Too often, winning becomes the god. Leo Durocher, a Hall of Fame baseball manager, put it this way: "If it's under W for win, nobody asks you how." But we know better. We know that God is just as concerned with our character as with how we do things.

How important is winning to some athletes? In his book *Death in the Locker Room*, Bob Goldman wrote: "I asked 198 top world-class athletes . . . 'If I had a magic drug that was so fantastic that if you took it once you would win every competition you would enter . . . [but] it would kill you five years after you took it, would you still take the drug?' Fifty-two percent said yes." That's a good example of a warped perspective: Winning overrides all other goals.

► The Athlete's Response

On the one hand, the Bible doesn't command you to hand up your uniform and enjoy "less

Attitude Scoreboard

How about your competitive mindset? For each sports-related situation, circle the number that best represents your answer. Discuss your answers with a friend.

1. All through a game, your opponents taunt and insult you. The opposing team wins. What do you do after the game?

1	2	3	4	5	6	7	8	9	10

Smile, shake hands and congratulate the other team.

Shake hands without smiling.

Ignore players from the other team.

2. You've surprised everyone by making the finals of the conference tennis tournament. You play the top seed and lose, 7-6, 7-5. How do you feel?

1	2	3	4	5	6	7	8	9	10

Disappointed, but pleased that you played so well and made it as far as you did.

A little sad that you made it so far, only to lose.

Angry at yourself for blowing key points and losing a match you should have won.

3. You have a chance to play on a county all-star soccer team. One catch: Practices are held on Sunday mornings. What do you do?

1	2	3	4	5	6	7	8	9	10

Turn it down and trust another opportunity will come along.

Try to strike a deal with the coach to make half the practices.

Join the all-star team.

What Does the Bible Say?

Read the following Bible passages and answer the questions:

1. "And Jesus grew in wisdom and stature, and in favor with God and men" (Luke 2:52). Do you think Jesus participated in sports as a child? as a teenager? as a young man? Why or why not?

2. "If anyone competes as an athlete, he does not receive the visitor's crown unless he competes according to the rules" (2 Timothy 2:5). How would you feel about a Christian athlete who takes steroids because they make him or her a better athlete? who intentionally breaks the rules because it helps him or her win?

3. "I have fought the good fight, I have finished the race, I have kept the faith. Now there is in store for me the crown of righteousness" (2 Timothy 4:7-8). In what ways does athletic discipline help you as a Christian?

worldly" pursuits. But on the other hand, be aware.

- Are you unable to compete without hating your opponent?
- Is your self-image tied to the outcome, so much that losing destroys you?
- Do sports come between you and God?

Christianity and sports can mix. But Christianity comes first. If you find you simply can't compete and reflect Christian character, it might be time to take a little time off and get that together.

But such instances are rare. Chances are, you can enjoy sports and please God at the same time. Just "go out there and give it all you've got" in both areas, and you'll come out a winner.

John Carvalho

Chapter 10

When the Future Scares You

How does God fit into your future?

Diane machine-gunned questions at me the minute we met. I didn't have a chance. Question after question after question. There was no time to respond to any of them.

"Does the Bible say the world will end in a ball of fire? Does that mean nuclear war will make the world go up in smoke? Is it normal to worry about these things? Am I crazy? Sometimes I just start crying and feel like I can't stop. Does anyone else feel like that?"

I quickly realized Diane wasn't just looking for answers about nuclear war or the end of the world. She needed relief from the internal pressure caused by her fear of the future. She also needed to know that she was okay even though she felt those pressures. But what could I say that would respect her feelings and also offer guidance?

As we talked, it became obvious that fear had been growing inside Diane for a long time. She suffered from a nagging feeling that something terrible was going to happen. But she didn't know exactly what caused her fear. When she looked at the future, she felt overwhelmed by the terrible things that might happen. She assaulted me with questions, hoping to find a path through the maze.

► Future Fears

It's not unusual to experience waves of anxiety about the future. Uncertainty peeks at us from every nook of the unknown. "Will I fail my driving test?" "What if she laughs in my face when I ask her out?" "What will I do after I graduate?" "How can I ever afford a house?" "What does God want me to do with my life?" "What would happen if my parents were killed in a traffic accident?"

Jesus advised us not to be anxious about our lives, but to allow God to be the Lord of our lives. Jesus reminded us that God always knows what we need. He'll provide us with the same opportunities for life and growth that he gives to the lilies of the field (Luke 12:22-31). But it's up to us to maintain our relationship with him. Even the lilies will shrivel and die without the nurturing foundation of the Earth and the life-sustaining water.

Unlike the lilies, though, we can experience fear and anxiety. These feelings are triggered by our awareness that we could choose to go against God's will. We fear the real possibility that we might not know his will completely enough to avoid going against it. We might make a mistake out of ignorance and foul everything up. We're not sure we have enough wisdom to make a creative choice that will keep us on God's paths.

► Unexpected Events

But what if something horrible does happen? Take Ronnie, for example. His dad suddenly died of a heart attack. Without warning, the family's future slid into uncertainty. Ronnie's dad had been a beacon and guide for Ronnie in discussing his life plans. The family's financial stability had depended on his father's income. Along with the personal loss of a loving father, Ronnie felt crushed by the weight of uncertainty.

Until his dad died, Ronnie had taken life almost casually. He achieved good grades fairly easily and always believed he could make it at the college level. He also worked part time after school and knew he could handle job responsibilities. The future didn't worry him too much, since he felt it would all work out. But with his father gone, nothing seemed certain anymore.

► Facing Fear

As we talked about the uncertainties surrounding his future, Ronnie began to see the scriptures

Your Future Career

"What do you want to be when you grow up?" That question was probably much easier for you to answer as a 5-year-old than it is today. There are so many options. Where do you start? Here are some steps to help:

- **Think about what you like to do.** What experiences have you had that might suggest a career direction? Use these questions to help you think about your preferences:
  - Do you like to be indoors or outdoors?
  - Would you like work that requires frequent contact with the public?
  - Is money an important factor in your decision?
  - Do you like to work with tools and machinery?
  - Would you enjoy work that requires great physical stamina?
  - Would you like work that requires problem-solving and creativity?
  - Do you enjoy doing things that are repetitious?
  - Would you enjoy detail or precision work?
  - Do you like to have influence over others?
- **Talk to a school guidance counselor.** When you've chosen a few fields to explore further, ask your counselor what types of jobs are available in those fields.

continued

For example, if you're good in English, you have many more options than being an English teacher. You could be a journalist or a news reporter, or you could learn another language and be a translator. Discover your options.

Ask your counselor where you can take a vocational aptitude test. This can confirm that your interests are your strengths—or it can open up new fields for you to think about.

- **Seek other people's advice.** Often those who live closest to you know you best. They know your likes and dislikes and, most of all, they care about your future. They may also be aware of a field you haven't even thought of. Let them know you're asking for advice—not for the final word on what you should do.

- **Visit colleges and vocational schools.** Not all careers require a college or vocational education. But if your interest does lead to further education, write for information from many schools that have programs you might consider. Then visit at least the one you're most interested in.

- **Pray for guidance.** God is involved in your career decision too. Ask other youth group members, your pastor and youth leader, your parents and family members to pray for you. And keep your career decision in your own prayers as well.

Margaret Hinchey

in a new way. Psalm 23 took on an intensely personal meaning as Ronnie related his experience to "the valley of the shadow of death" (Psalm 23:4). He became aware that God's presence made a big difference in his attitude, and he started to develop confidence as he faced the unknown. Ronnie began to chip away at his fears.

Gradually, Ronnie realized God would be with him in the future, just as he was with him in the present. And Ronnie's anxiety about the future caused him to ask questions that led him closer to God.

One day, Ronnie exploded into my office grinning from ear to ear. He had discovered Isaiah. He felt that Isaiah was speaking directly to him when he read: "Fear not, for I am with you. Be not dismayed, for I am your God; I will strengthen you, I will help you, I will uphold you with my victorious right hand" (Isaiah 41:10). This passage brought all his scripture studies together.

It was almost as if Ronnie had found his father alive in the back yard. Once again, there was guidance and support in his life. Ronnie knew there would be surprises in the future, but he felt confident that Someone was walking alongside him as he made his choices.

Ronnie knew his answers were not complete. His direction was not entirely clear. But he felt once again he had a personal relationship that would help him in the struggle to find answers. He wasn't alone. Now he felt confident to face the future and take one step at a time in working it out.

When we realize we have freedom to choose,

we can feel afraid and anxious. Surprisingly, the fact that we're created in God's image places us in this fearful position. We have the freedom to operate like God, to make decisions from unlimited choices. But because God has given us complete freedom to make these choices, we also can make big mistakes.

We can make destructive choices, ruining our opportunities for completeness and fulfillment. In these choices, anxiety builds. Fear of the future grows out of our fear of making the wrong choices.

► Wiping Out Worries

A personal relationship with God can furnish a new point of view about mistakes and problems. So, if you're worried about getting laughed at when you ask someone for a date, you can have more freedom from fear. With God by your side, you can put the situation in true perspective. You can take a more lighthearted approach if she or he turns you down. You can think to yourself, "With God and me as a team, we'll be a great date for someone else!"

Or, if you fail a drivers test, you can always look at it as a learning experience, not the final word about your ability to drive. "What can I learn from this test that will make me a better driver?" "Maybe God wants me to be safer before I start driving, since he probably has plans for me that don't include traffic accidents."

That's why we need to keep God's Word, particularly through the life of Jesus Christ, fresh in our minds and hearts. God's perspective on life leads us through our fears and restores our souls.

Living with God's Word wraps us in the assurance of his care, even though we don't know everything about God. Reading from his Word daily covers us with a sense of his love and acceptance.

We won't worry as much about mistakes and wrong choices because we know we have a friend who will help us as we work on our problems. We can live with the belief that God will guide us now and in the future because we feel him with us.

John Shaw

Part Two

Making Room for God

Chapter 11

Tuning in to God

Making room for God by learning to listen

When was the last time God handed you Ten Commandments cut in stone (Deuteronomy 5)?

When was the last time you had a one-to-one conversation with God while walking in a garden (Genesis 3)?

Can you remember the last time you hung out with Jesus, Moses and Elijah (Mark 9)?

Or the last time God spoke to you directly (1 Kings 19)?

If you're having trouble remembering these incidents, you may also be asking yourself, "How in the world does God speak to me?"

► When God Talks, People Listen

In the Bible, God talks to people left and right. You can hardly read more than a page or two without God having some sort of personal conversation with somebody. God makes a personal appearance to talk with Isaiah about his career as a prophet in Isaiah 6. God discusses with Abraham about whether or not to nuke Sodom (Genesis 18). And God has a heart-to-heart talk with Saul on the road to Damascus in Acts 9.

When God isn't talking to somebody in the Bible, you find the apostles experiencing the Holy Spirit in Acts 2. Or you read people's stories of visions of God in great detail in the books of Revelation and Daniel.

But what about today? How does God talk to you?

► Tuning in to KGOD

Hearing God's voice is as simple as tuning a radio to your favorite channel. Once you've learned to tune in to Channel KGOD, you can receive God's message in the Bible, in music, in the voices of friends, in a sunset, in church, while riding in a car or standing on your head.

How do you tune in to God? Start by clearing away some of the clutter in your life. Learn how to feel. The biggies in the Bible—from Adam to John—each heard God's voice by opening their heart and soul to God.

► Listening to the Bible

People will tell you that God speaks through the Bible. They're right. But sometimes it's tough to wade through the Bible. That can make it tough to hear God's voice.

But don't give up. It's not that God doesn't speak to you through the Bible; it's more a problem of learning how to listen.

The most important thing to remember about reading the Bible is don't just read it. If you just read the Bible, you might as well read the Sunday comics.

Instead, try *feeling* the Bible. And I don't mean picking it up and tossing it around in your hands. Get in touch with your feelings as you read the Bible. Put yourself in the Bible.

Take the story of the good Samaritan in Luke 10:30-37. The next time you read it, put yourself in the story. Walk a few steps behind the Samaritan and ask yourself: What am I feeling, hearing, tasting, smelling and seeing? How does it feel to walk on that long, hot, dusty road? How do I feel when I see other people pass by the guy who just got mugged? How do I feel when I see the Samaritan stop, take care of the guy and put him on his donkey? How do I feel when the Samaritan gives the innkeeper some money to take care of the guy?

Bring the story to life in your heart. The minute you let yourself become a part of the story, you open your heart to God. And God has a chance to talk to you. When you come at the Bible with your feelings, everything changes.

Suddenly Luke 22:47-48, in which Judas betrays Jesus with a kiss, becomes your story. You feel the pain and disappointment of being betrayed. And God can speak to you about the betrayals in your life.

All of Job's pain and anguish about feeling

abandoned by God become your feelings of loneliness and abandonment. "Where is God?" becomes a real and personal question. And the minute you ask it, you may open yourself to experiencing your deepest feelings. Then God has a great opportunity in chapters 38—41 to tell you that he is always present.

► Listening for God's Voice

What's tough about trying to hear God's voice is the distractions. Commercials try to lure us to buy products. We hear messages such as: "Drive the right car." "Wear the right clothes." "Do what everybody else is doing."

Yes, listening to God's voice in this noisy world is tough. But it is possible. The key is to listen to your heart—not to what MTV, ABC, NBC, CBS, CNN or HBO say.

So how does God speak? It depends. You may hear God speaking to you through your heart:

- in a beautiful sunrise or sunset.
- in your favorite piece of music.
- in that strange reading assignment your English teacher gave you that suddenly makes sense.
- when a friend needs someone to talk to. And you say the right thing.
- when someone forgives you for something you figured would be unforgivable.
- when you forgive somebody you thought you could never forgive.
- when you share with a friend a secret that's been weighing you down.

Your Faith Tuneup

Sometimes we treat our faith like an old car. We depend on it to get us where we need to go. But we don't pay much attention to it until something goes wrong. Then we need an overhaul, not just a tuneup. Here's a checklist and diagnostic chart to help you keep your faith in tune now so you won't need a tow truck later on.

Answer the following questions:

	Always	Sometimes	Never
1. Do I take responsibility for my faith?	☐	☐	☐
2. Do I surround myself with Christian friends?	☐	☐	☐
3. Do I get involved in the Bible?	☐	☐	☐
4. Do I worship regularly?	☐	☐	☐
5. Do I give myself away by doing things for others?	☐	☐	☐
6. Do I pray and trust God will support me?	☐	☐	☐
7. Do I look for results of faith in my relationships?	☐	☐	☐

Diagnostic Chart

1. Do I take responsibility for my faith? Other people aren't to blame for your lack of growth. The fault doesn't lie in an unsupportive family, non-Christian friends, an unexciting youth leader or boring church services. Realize that you—and only you—are responsible for your personal faith life.

2. Do I surround myself with Christian friends? It's important to be in healthy relationships with other Christians. By consciously choosing to be with people who share the faith, you help support one another.

3. Do I get involved in the Bible? Daily personal Bible reading and devotions are terrific for your faith growth. Not only is it a learning process, it's a way of saying you're serious about your commitment to grow.

Also join a weekly Bible study. Make it a point to take part and ask questions. Don't be afraid to admit that you don't know everything. People who already know everything don't need a Bible class.

4. Do I worship regularly? People who don't go to church miss a valuable source of strength and energy. Christians *need* a community of people who share the common bond of faith. A date once a week with God and his people isn't too much to ask. Worship is your opportunity to praise, thank, confess and pray.

5. Do I give myself away by doing things for others? There's something wonderfully strange about faith and love: The more you give away, the more you have. All the Bible studies and prayer meetings in the world have little effect unless you *do* something. Volunteer to serve on the

continued

youth council; wash Grandma Smith's windows; give the church 10 percent of the money you earn; or be a candy striper at a hospital. The opportunities for giving yourself away are unlimited.

6. Do I pray and trust God will support me? Ask God to work the miracle of faith within you. He promises to hold you, support you and care for you—no matter what! Take advantage of that loyal friendship.

7. Do I look for results of faith in my relationships? After you've started practicing and living your faith, you'll find that giving and loving are enjoyable. No doubt people will notice there's something peculiarly special about you. The brilliancy of Christ's light shining through you is too powerful to go unseen. By giving without expectation, loving unconditionally and forgiving freely, you'll discover the joy and rewards of a growing faith.

Completing the Tuneup

Now look at your faith checkup. What areas need the most improvement? Think of one thing you can do this week to move you into faith action.

Make sure you can answer yes to these three questions about your goal:

- Is it possible and realistic?
- Is it specific and measurable?
- Is it something you have complete control over?

Write your goal here:

Joani Schultz

► Taking Time to Listen

God's voice can get crowded out by all the stuff that fills our lives. That's why it's important to take some time out. You can do this by considering the following:

- Pray.
- Once you've finished praying, stop and listen to hear whether God has anything to say.
- If you're not praying, sit quietly and imagine that Christ is gently pouring water on your head out of his cupped hands. How do you feel?
- Take a long walk and imagine Christ walking with you. What is he saying to you? Or is he simply walking with you in loving silence?

If you're not praying, meditating or taking long walks, try this: Put an ice cube in a metal pot. Put the pot on the stove and turn the stove on high. Now watch the ice cube turn to water. Then to steam. And finally disappear.

Think of the miracle that has just happened. You've taken something solid, watched it turn to liquid then disappear. But it didn't really disappear. Somewhere, sometime, it will fall to Earth again as water or snow and the circle of creation will begin again.

Sure it's only physics. At least that's what your mind may say. But your heart may say something else. Your heart may feel that if God loves the water so much that it never really disappears, how much more must God love you.

Learning to listen to your heart as well as your head is the first step to hearing God's voice in your life. So take the time. Listen.

Jim Smith-Farris

Chapter 12

Does God Really Answer My Prayers?

Making room for God through prayer

Living in the Chicago area, I spent part of a summer afternoon watching a Cubs game on television. In the middle of a close game, the Cubs had runners on base and my hero, Ernie Banks, came to bat.

In a sudden fervor, I knelt down and prayed for a home run. Then I sat back again feeling sure it would happen. I could see it in my mind. I expected it with each pitch.

And it happened!

Today when I see Ernie Banks' stats of 512 home runs, I say semiseriously, "One of those is mine."

A little later, my cat ran away. He was ugly, old and beaten up. But he was the only pet I'd ever owned. My whole life turned into shambles. So I prayed.

And in prayer, I remembered a lie I'd recently told. I confessed the lie. That evening the cat returned.

Whoa! I felt like Midas after he discovered he had the touch.

Then my grandmother became ill. So I prayed. And in prayer, I remembered a small tool I'd stolen from shop class. I returned the tool and confessed what I'd done to Wild Bull Larson, the shop teacher. Wild Bull shook his head, mumbled something and probably figured the Anderson kid had finally lost it.

That weekend my grandmother died.

So does God answer prayer?

Always? Sometimes? Never?

► Prayer Puzzlers

What does Jesus say about prayer? I've always been intrigued with the story Jesus told about prayer. He put it this way:

" 'Ask, and you will receive; seek, and you will find; knock, and the door will be opened to you. For everyone who asks will receive, and anyone who seeks will find, and the door will be opened to him who knocks. Would any of you who are fathers give your son a stone when he asks for bread? Or would you give him a snake when he asks for a fish? As bad as you are, you know how to give good things to your children. How much more, then, will your Father in heaven give good things to those who ask him!' " (Matthew 7:7-11).

Who Prayed for What?

People throughout the Bible prayed to God. And they hoped God would answer their prayers. Sometimes God said yes. Other times he said no.

Read the statements below. Figure out who in the Bible made these requests:

1. Who prayed for his friends?

2. Who prayed that the thorn in his flesh be removed?

3. Who prayed for strength?

4. Who prayed to "let this cup pass"?

5. Who prayed in anger for the Lord to take his life away?

6. Who prayed about himself?

Answers: 1. Job (Job 42:10). 2. Paul (2 Corinthians 12:7-9). 3. Samson (Judges 16:28). 4. Jesus (Matthew 26:39, 42, 44). 5. Jonah (Jonah 4:1-4). 6. The Pharisee (Luke 18:11).

Improving Your Prayer Life

Every time you turn around, somebody's saying we need to pray more. And most of us *want* to spend more time in prayer, but we just can't seem to be consistent at it. Here are some practical suggestions to help you set aside quality time with God.

- **Find a place** to be your "prayer closet." It could be a nearby park, your church sanctuary or even your bedroom closet.
- **Write a list** of things you want to pray for—your family, friends, teachers, pastor, youth group. Also list special needs as they come up.
- **Commit to a daily time.** Schedule the same time for prayer every day if possible. However, your Monday through Friday schedule is probably different from Saturday and Sunday. *When* you pray isn't as important as taking the time to pray.
- **Read about prayer.** There are many books on prayer, not to mention the great prayers of the Bible. Read the Psalms. Ask your youth leader or pastor to recommend a good book on prayer.
- **Ask God to make your prayer time effective** and meaningful. You'll soon enjoy your prayer time and look forward to it.
- **Keep a journal.** Record your special prayers, answered prayers and other meaningful thoughts about prayer. Regularly reflect on your writings.
- **Take time to listen** to God. Be still before the Lord. As you read your Bible, expect God to speak to you.
- **Realize what a privilege** prayer is. Think of prayer as your 800 number to heaven. It's toll free, always works and is never busy, and you don't get an answering machine.

Buddy Duncan

At times I think I'm an easy parent. I enjoy giving things to my children and making them happy. So sometimes I struggle to say no. I know now, however, that I'm just a poor imitation of a giving father compared with the heavenly Father.

God loves nothing more than giving good things to his children. And the best gift he loves to give—more than any other—is the gift of his lordship. God wants us to trust him completely. He wants us not to restrict ourselves to our own abilities to find happiness.

One of the most loving things God does is *not* answering all my prayers according to my wishes. If he did, then he wouldn't be God but a rabbit's foot or a puppet, something under my control. In that case, the happiness and goodness of my life would only be as good as I could understand it and make it.

If God became a god in which we rubbed his belly and our wishes came true, our prayers would serve only our egos and self-will. And that'd be a terribly unloving thing for God to do. It'd be like parents giving their children a snake when they asked for food.

► Prayer Pointers

So how should we pray? And what should we expect? Try these ideas:

• ***Pray to Abba.*** In the New Testament, this Aramaic word always gets translated "Father." But that's not accurate. In English, we have many words for our male parent—Father, Dad, Daddy. The same is true in Aramaic.

So translate Abba as Daddy. Jesus himself prayed to Abba. It's the most childlike and intimate of all prayer forms. And it best expresses how we should approach God.

● ***Pray prayers you know God can't resist answering.*** Then picture God hearing and responding.

Pray: "Lord, I want to learn your will. Would you help me?" "I want to know how to be your child. Please help me."

When I'm frustrated and don't know where to go for help, the only prayer I know is "God, love me." How could an Abba resist such a prayer?

● ***Ask the Holy Spirit to pray for you.*** I often confess I don't know what to ask or even hope for. Then I sit in silence. I open my hands before God and ask the Holy Spirit to lift up my life.

This is an act of surrender. And it's often the most powerful part of my prayer life. Then I usually go on, not so much with a clearer understanding of God's care, but with a deeper trust and assurance in it.

The most beautiful process of prayer—and of life—isn't getting what I ask for, but the process of day-by-day surrendering myself to God's care, whether I understand it or not. Through this process, I learn that God always answers prayer. Maybe not in the way I'd always like him to. But he *always* answers prayer.

Timothy R. Anderson

Chapter 13

Is the "Good Book" Any Good?

Making room for God through Bible study

Picture this: Sixteen-year-old Wally clears his throat. He's about to lead his first Bible study for the youth group. He begins to speak.

"In the Bible, you can find lots of examples on how to live as a Christian. Take Abraham, for example. He was called God's friend. Why? Because Abraham believed God and did what God wanted.

"Abraham traveled around following God, living in tents and marrying women."

Then Wally smiles.

"Now we must not let anything keep us from following Abraham's example. We must live in tents. We must travel around. We must have at least two wives."

Is that what the Bible *really* says? Or is Wally

implying that the Bible, a book that's so old and describes a primitive culture, seems irrelevant?

Wally is probably like a lot of us. He gets stuck looking at the Bible's cultural details rather than seeing the timeless truths embedded in those old stories.

► A Book of Faith

So what is the Bible? What does it really have to say to us? The Bible is a "faith book." A book packed with God's never-ending faith in his people as they journey toward faith in him. It tells Israel's story and the Israelites' walk of faith with God. The Good Book tells the good news of salvation, Christ's life, death and Resurrection. It shows real people's faith journeys—their ups *and* downs.

But the Bible is even more than a faith book. Its pages sparkle with history, ethics, theology, love stories, poetry, hymns, allegories—all kinds of stuff.

But regardless of the kind of literature found in the Bible, it's essentially irrelevant if you don't believe that the Bible is God's Word. Paul wrote to Timothy, "All Scripture is inspired by God and is useful for teaching the truth" (2 Timothy 3:16). In order for the Bible to be relevant to us, we need to accept, by faith, that the Bible is a message to us from God's heart.

► A Book for the People

That still doesn't show any connections with

Choosing a Bible

You want a good Bible. So you go to your local bookstore to pick one up. But when you reach the Bible section, you see rows and rows of Bibles. You ask the salesperson which is best. He asks whether you want an RSV, TEV, NEB, NKJV, KJV, NIV or NASB version. You wonder what he's talking about. You feel like one of the Israelites wandering in the wilderness.

There certainly are a lot of choices. Let's look at the different options.

- **Translations.** Scholars have been translating the Bible for centuries. Early in the 17th century, King James I of England put about 50 Greek and Hebrew scholars to work to translate

continued

what we know as the King James Version (KJV).

The King James Version was written in the way English people spoke in 1611. That's quite different from the way North Americans (and even English people) speak today. Christians want a Bible that's easy to understand. When people use the King James Version translation today, they need to know that in the 1600s "suffer" meant "allow" and "allow" meant "approve."

Because language changes, we need new Bible versions to keep the Bible in the language of the people. Three recent translations that were carefully done and widely accepted are the Revised Standard Version (RSV), Today's English Version (TEV) and the New International Version (NIV).

● **Paraphrases.** Translating the Bible into words people can understand isn't always easy. So some people paraphrase the Bible—rewriting passages in ways that directly address contemporary people.

The most popular paraphrase Bible is the Living Bible (LB). The person who developed this paraphrase took an English translation and tried to make it simpler and clearer. He wanted to put the *meaning* of the

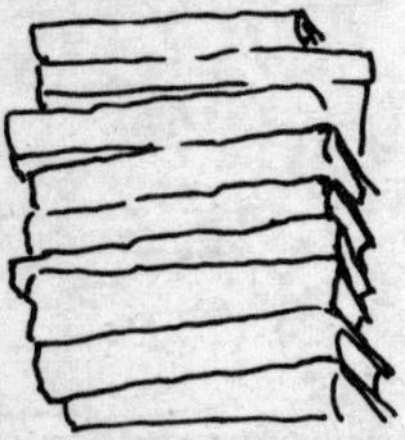

continued

Bible into today's language.

But paraphrases sometimes change and add to God's message. So while paraphrases are enjoyable to read, you need to use an accurate translation as your standard Bible.

● **Special features.** Many Bibles also include other features such as study notes, Jesus' words in red, illustrations, maps and references. These special features can help you understand God's message.

Some denominations use Bibles with particular notes. A few years ago, most Catholics used a Douay-Rheims translation of the Latin Bible with notes. So find out what translation your denomination emphasizes. That will help you understand the differences in the notes and study helps.

So before you buy a Bible, think through the different features available. And if you choose a paraphrase, also buy at least one standard translation to use.

Select a Bible *you* will use. A Bible that sits on the shelf doesn't communicate God's message. And communicating God's message is what Bibles are for.

Eldor Kaiser

life in the late 20th century. If the Bible is relevant today, why doesn't it talk about birth control, peer pressure, working part time and getting good grades?

One of my youth group members had an answer. "The situation 2,000 years ago was different from today, but the people were essentially the same as we are. They felt lonely, we feel lonely. They disobeyed God, we disobey God. They wanted to be loved, we want to be loved."

I liked that answer. Whether I'm a first-century tent maker or a 20th-century computer programmer, I still struggle with relationships. I still sin, and I still need God.

Maybe people haven't changed much since biblical times, but the situations sure have. Unfortunately it's easy to focus on the historical situations in the Bible and miss the point. And if you get hung up on those differences, you'll wonder how the Bible means anything today.

► A Guidebook

When you start reading the Bible more, you'll see that it does have meaning. Let's look at some timeless truths the Bible tells that speak to today's issues:

- ***On getting caught.*** You can't get more ancient than Adam and Eve. In Genesis 3, they chose to disobey God, and they immediately felt embarrassed and guilty. When they heard their Creator walking around in the garden, they hid themselves. When God found them, God asked Adam why they were hiding. Adam said he felt afraid because he was naked. Have you ever felt embarrassed and afraid when you were caught doing something you knew was wrong?

● ***On peer pressure.*** You're at a party and the beer is flowing like Niagara Falls. A friend offers you a drink. Enter: peer pressure!

What does the Bible say about peer pressure? More than you think. Look at Aaron in Exodus 32, for example. He got stuck with a lot of restless people while his brother Moses had been gone a long time. The people wanted some religious action. Aaron, who was left in charge, knew that things were getting out of hand. The people asked Aaron to make an idol for them to worship instead of worshiping God. Enter: peer pressure!

● ***On AIDS.*** Jesus encountered a group of people considered unclean and untouchable in Luke 17:11-19. They had a contagious disease called leprosy, which many people believed was caused by sin. Jesus treated these people with compassion, and on several occasions physically touched them.

In some ways, AIDS victims are today's lepers. Yes, many who have the disease contracted it because they chose a high-risk lifestyle. But others who suffer from this disease contracted it innocently. The Bible encourages us to be like Jesus, who touched the untouchable and loved the unlovable.

● ***On rock music.*** There was a problem in Corinth. In 1 Corinthians 8, we read about some church people buying and eating meat that had been offered to idols. Other people thought that was bad news. They said buying and eating that meat approved of idol worship.

Today some Christians think listening to contemporary Christian artists is like worshiping idols. They're convinced that rock music—Christian or otherwise—is evil. But other Christians disagree. They feel Christian musicians sing worthwhile songs. Read 1 Corinthians 8 to get Paul's solution to the problem.

How relevant is the Bible today? Plenty. Downright essential. But it will take time in prayer, thought and careful study to find out how directly the Bible speaks to us today. And the payoff is worth the effort.

Bob Searl

Bits About the Bible

Since the Bible is a best seller, many publishers print lots of Bible variations. Did you know:

- More than 60 companies publish Bibles.
- You can choose from more than 2,670 different Bibles.
- There have been more than 250 different Bible editions translated into English since 1611. At least 34 translations are still available today.
- There are at least a dozen different Bibles written just for teenagers.
- You can pay more than $100 for a gold-leaf, leather-bound Bible.
- The King James Version is the best-selling Bible.
- Cambridge University Press has been printing Bibles since 1591.
- At least parts of the Bible have been translated into more than 1,700 languages.
- More than 90 percent of the world's population has the entire Bible translated into its own language.

Eldor Kaiser

Chapter 14

Do I Have to Go to Church?

Making room for God through church attendance

I'm a preacher's kid. I had to go to church. But I didn't always want to. I protested by playing tick-tack-toe on the church bulletin. I shaped other bulletins into Lear jets and launched them from the balcony.

I conjured up excuses for not going to church. "Hey, Mom," I yelled from my bed on Sunday morning, "what does it mean when the right half of your body goes numb?"

► Excuses, Excuses

You probably know of better, prize-winning excuses. You may keep a long list of moans and groans. Do any of these sound familiar?

• ***"Church is boring."*** Most churches don't have video games and a Ferris wheel. Every part of church is boring sometimes. And some parts of church seem boring all the time. Of course, the same can be said for school, work and parades.

If you find church boring, make it less so. Your involvement can beat the boredom. An active youth group can make church more exciting for everyone. You can do what Acts 20:28 says.

Because people make up the church, they bring their strengths and weaknesses. Not every pastor can keep the members on the edge of their pews. He or she may be better at administration or counseling.

But the pastor isn't the church. *You* are the church. If church bores you, find ways to jazz it up. Offer suggestions. Volunteer your energy and enthusiasm. Give your church everything you've got. You'll be amazed how boring can turn into soaring.

• ***"Church doesn't relate to life."*** Did you ever hear a joke that wasn't funny until the punch line hit you later? Church is like that. You won't always bounce out the church doors on Sunday morning feeling spiritually revved up. In fact, you may leave wondering why you bothered going at all.

Sooner or later something will click inside your head. That sermon, Bible story or Sunday morning worship experience will speak directly to you. And it will be jampacked with meaning.

• ***"Hypocrites make up the church."*** Not only does the church have hypocrites, it also has liars, warmongers, thieves, swindlers and your typical commandment-busters. If you're not a hypocrite or a sinner, don't go near a church. Someone once said: "Don't stay away from church because there are so many hypocrites. There's always room for one more."

Like Matthew 9:12 says, Christ didn't establish the church for the pure and saintly. Christ extended his invitation to the sinful, the hurting, the broken. It's like your doctor's office; it isn't full of well people.

● ***"I can worship God in other ways."*** I've felt close to God while sitting on a rock in the middle of a mountain stream. I've felt spiritually refreshed while hiking through secluded woods.

But I also believe you miss out on a vital part of the Christian experience if you skip church. At church, you can interact with God and other people. Your church is made up of a worshiping, praying, talking, laughing, listening, learning, responding family of God.

Jesus wasn't a loner. At times, he went off by himself. But he always returned to be with people. Christianity, after all, should be a verb. And an active verb is stronger than a passive one.

● ***"Church doesn't hit current issues."*** The church tends to drag its feet when it comes to getting involved in contemporary issues. Some Christians even believe the church ought to avoid worldly matters altogether.

A church gets involved in current affairs to the extent that its people get involved. If you think your church lives in the '50s, help your church get current. Your youth group can clear away the church's cobwebs. All you have to do is get involved. Create worship ideas. And do them.

- ***"Others don't go. Why should I?"*** Your friends may not go to church. Your parents might not either. But don't stay away from church for other people's reasons. Stand on your own feet. Do what you want to do.

Get involved. Have a ball. Meet new friends. And you'll make a difference.

- ***"Church starts too early."*** So does the sunrise. But isn't it gorgeous?

► Church Is Important

The church is like a pair of shoes. Walk in it. If it feels comfortable, stick with it. If not, find a pair that fits. There's a size and style for everyone.

If we're not involved in church, I believe we're missing a vital element of the Christian life. The worshiping fellowship of Christians is essential to living a full, Christ-centered life.

But church attendance doesn't make a Christian, just like owning a violin doesn't make you a violinist. You'll never become a good violinist if you just fiddle around with the instrument whenever you feel like it instead of practicing regularly.

A friend of mine believes that going to a Weight Watchers meeting is like going to church. When she goes to the meetings, she sees friends who are also overweight.

They understand her frustrations and her wild eating binges. They experience the same frustrations and anxieties. She admits she probably couldn't lose all the weight by herself. She needs the encouragement of those around her. And they need her encouragement.

So, go. Get involved. Give yourself the honor and privilege of enriching your life and the lives of others. Forget your list of excuses.

Give church a chance. Bring your flaws, doubts and shortcomings. I'll be there with mine. And we'll both meet some of the finest, imperfect people on Earth.

Tom Tozer

Your Church's Job Description

What can you contribute? Don't wait for the church to think of some ideas. Think of your own.

In the space below, write a job description for your church by ranking its five major job responsibilities. (Read these Bible passages to get you started: Psalms 95:6-7; 118:24; 133:1; Proverbs 18:24; 29:18; Matthew 10: 8, 34; John 5:39; Romans 12:10; 1 Corinthians 13:3; and 1 John 4:7.)

Your church's job responsibilities:

1.

2.

3.

4.

5.

Next, imagine you're applying for a job at your church. Rank your five top talents or skills and write them below.

My five top talents or skills:

1.

2.

3.

4.

5.

Now match your skills with the five most important job responsibilities of the church. Do any match? If so, congratulations. You get the job. Volunteer your services and get busy. You and your church may need each other more than you think.

Afterword

What Does God Expect?

The king was going to sail in a small ship. A crowd waited for him and his party to ride down to the dock. Finally they came. A small young man named Almost stood on his toes in the crowd trying to see.

Finally he got a glimpse of the king. Almost was excited. And then Almost noticed the king's horse. He was a beauty. His golden mane shimmered in the sun. The horse held his head high. Almost thought he was perfect in every way.

The king said he needed someone to take his horse to the palace. He looked at Almost. "You, young man, take my horse to the palace." Before Almost knew what happened, he was holding the horse's reins and some money. The king was gone.

Almost looked at the horse. He realized he'd been given a great responsibility.

God gives you gifts—talents, abilities, opportu-

nities. They're all perfect. But they aren't really yours. God gives them to you to use on your journey through life. And sometimes those demands seem scary and overwhelming.

Proudly, Almost led the king's horse through the village streets and country roads. He couldn't think of riding him. He was afraid if he did, the horse wouldn't be in perfect condition when he delivered him to the king.

Are you ever afraid to use the gifts God's given you? When you expect perfection, it may be scary to use your talents. But think about what the master said to the servant who buried his one talent (Matthew 25:25-28).

► When Life Gets Rough

After a few days, the countryside became rugged. Almost and the horse came to a deep gorge with a roaring river. Almost looked for a bridge. But there was none. And no one was around to help. Almost sat down on a rock. What could he do?

The horse gently nuzzled Almost under his arm. Then Almost heard a muffled voice say, "Ride me." Almost looked around. No one was there.

Almost jumped onto the horse. And they plunged into the raging river. But by midstream, Almost panicked. The water washed over them both. Almost came up coughing. He clung to the horse for life.

Eventually they made it to the other side of the river. Almost looked at the horse. He was exhausted and caked with mud. Almost felt miserable. Then he saw the blood. It was oozing from a long scratch across the horse's coat. Even if it healed well, the coat would never again be perfect. Almost felt like a failure.

Do you think you're a failure when you don't do something perfectly? What do you think God expects of you? In Matthew 5:48, Jesus says, "You must be perfect—just as your Father in heaven is perfect." Does God expect the impossible from you?

Some Christians try hard to do everything right. They start out trying to please their parents. And they wind up trying to please everybody. That's the impossible bind that trying to be perfect can get you into.

► When You Try Hard

The horse looked so bad that no one knew he belonged to the king. And Almost had lost the money in the river. The horse needed hay and rest. To get money, Almost entered a horse race at a county fair. He thought he could win.

On the last lap, Almost's foot slipped out of the stirrup. The horse instinctively slowed down. And they lost the race. Almost cried.

"Why do I always ruin everything? I couldn't even win a simple race with the best horse in the kingdom!"

Do you think you always need to win? Can you only please God by being the perfect athlete, student, musician or class president? Is that what being perfect means?

Lots of voices tell you to win in everything you do. Some may sound like the voice of God because they come from parents, coaches and teachers. Logic says: "God demands that I be perfect. So if I'm perfect, I'll always be a winner." But what kind of perfection does God want?

The discouraged horse and Almost continued their journey. Then they heard voices in the woods. They walked closer. They saw men trying to free a man's legs trapped under a fallen tree. No one could move the log.

Almost hitched the horse to the tree with a chain. The horse pulled and pulled. He stretched until his nose almost scraped the ground. Slowly the log rolled over. Everyone cheered. And Almost beamed. The horse was a hero.

The next day, Almost saw the horse limping. Almost stopped and let the horse rest. But the limping became worse. And Almost cried. He hugged the great steed's head and sobbed: "Why did this have to happen? Just when I thought we'd done something right, everything's a mess."

When you think you need to be perfect, you begin to want everything to turn out right. And when things don't, you may feel like a failure. You may blame yourself, others or even God. But nobody's perfect. Look at Romans 3:9-10 to see why.

► When You Fear the Worst

Finally Almost and the horse arrived at the palace. The gatekeeper let them into the yard. Al-

Realistic Expectations

Rate the expectations below. For each, mark an X on the spot on the continuum that indicates where you think that expectation best fits in your own experience.

Expectation	Too High	Right On	Too Low
1. To get grades only good enough to graduate.	●	●	●
2. To not go to the high school dance because you don't want to.	●	●	●
3. To make your parents proud of you.	●	●	●
4. To do the best you can.	●	●	●

Expectations vary from person to person. How did you rate the above expectations? For most, #1 would be too low. For #2, some may think it's right on. Others may believe it's an excuse because the real reason may be a fear of dating. The answers to #3 and #4 will vary, depending on how much pressure you put on yourself.

Share your answers with close friends. Talk about the differences. Discuss your expectations.

most slipped the halter off the horse and turned him loose. But Almost was afraid of what the king would say. So he tried to sneak away. But the king was standing there. "Well done, young man," the king said with a smile.

What happened? What's this about being perfect? It's true God demands you to be perfect. But Romans 5:8 shows that God loves you even though you're not perfect. God gives those who love him his perfect son. That's the only way you can be perfect.

The words in Matthew 5:48 suggest that God gives you the power for the perfection he demands. So in order for that to happen, you only need to accept the perfect life of Christ.

The perfection the law demands is to be sinless. And that shouldn't be confused with always being a winner or being the best. First Corinthians 4:2 says your role as a student, son, daughter, athlete, friend, class treasurer or whatever is to be faithful.

Faithfulness includes using your gifts to help others as well as yourself. And to give God the glory. Sometimes you won't win. Sometimes you'll mess up. But your king is gracious. And his grace makes you a winner.

Eldor Kaiser